Monet

Monet

Vanessa Potts

Introduction
by Dr Claire O'Mahony

This is a Parragon Publishing Book
This edition published in 2005

Parragon Publishing
Queen Street House
4 Queen Street
Bath BA1 1HE, UK

Printed and bound in China

contents

introd

C LAUDE OSCAR MONET is in many senses the quintessential Impressionist painter. The spontaneity and vivacity of his painting technique and his devotion to the close observation of nature have been the focus of most discussions of his art. However, the range of his subject matter, the complexities of his exhibiting strategies, and his responses to the variety of artistic and socio-historical transformations experienced during his long lifetime are fundamental to understanding his unique contribution to the history of art.

Born in 1840 in Paris, where his father was a wholesale grocer, Monet lived in Le Havre from the age of five; the Normandy region was to be a vital influence on him throughout his life. His earliest artistic reputation was as a caricaturist, but by the mid-1850s Monet, with the encouragement of the atmospheric landscape painter Eugène Boudin (1824–98), had begun to paint from the motif in the open air.

Monet's artistic career began in earnest with his first trip to Paris in 1859. On his arrival in the capital he was befriended by a number of painters associated with the Realist movement, most notably the Barbizon painter Constant Troyton (1810–65) and the young Camille Pissarro (1830–1903). He also received

A Corner of the Artist's Studio

uction

his first formal training, becoming a pupil for two years in the studio of the academic painter Charles Gleyre (1808–74). It was there that he made a number of artistic friendships that were to have a formative influence on him; he met Pierre-Auguste Renoir (1841–1919), Frédéric Bazille (1841–70), and Alfred Sisley (1839–99).

Despite legends stating the contrary, Monet had a degree of success at provincial exhibitions as well as at the annual State-

The Cart

sponsored art exhibition held in Paris each year in May, the Salon. In 1865, having made painting trips to the forest of Fontainebleau and the Normandy coast at Honfleur and Le Havre, where he met the Dutch open-air landscape painter Johan Barthold Jongkind (1819–91), Monet sent two of his seascapes to the Salon exhibition, and they were accepted. A portrait of his mistress, Camille Doncieux, and a landscape were also accepted in 1866 and another seascape in 1868.

Inspired in part by the controversial paintings Edouard Manet (1832–83) was

Fishing Boats, Honfleur

producing in the last years of the 1860s, Monet began to wrestle with subjects derived from the modern life of Paris. The capital had been undergoing a process of extraordinary transformation on the initiative of Emperor Napoleon III's prefect, Baron Haussmann. "Haussmannization" cut a series of huge boulevards, lined with large-scale expensive apartment blocks and arcades of stores,

Boulevard des Capucines

through the city's labyrinthine medieval streets, so beloved of an earlier generation of Romantic poets and artists. These changes necessitated the transplantation of the workers of Paris—who had lived in small upper rooms of the old buildings above the more lavish apartments of wealthier Parisians —to a new region of suburbs beyond the city walls. Monet, like many artists of the Impressionist circle, became fascinated with both the new phenomena of boulevard culture and the suburban districts, in which many pleasure spots blossomed alongside the factories on the banks of the River Seine.

Monet's technique and style reflect a wonderful awareness of the achievements of his teachers and contemporaries while also creating a unique and constantly transforming personal vision. The young Monet synthesized the open-air techniques practiced by Boudin and Jongkind and theorized by the drawing master Lecoq de Boisbaudran with the controversial subject matter of modern experience. The more abrupt handling and traditional palette of his earliest works were derived from the manner of Realist painters such as Gustave Courbet

(1819–77) and followers of the Barbizon School. In the following decades, Monet moved away from the traditional modeling in black and white, known as chiaroscuro, to a sense of depth and volume created entirely through color relationships. Rather than continuing to use the dark reddish-brown underpainting typical of the nineteenth century, Monet began to paint on canvases primed in white or light beige tones to enhance the brilliance of his colors.

Monet experimented with varying degrees of finish throughout his career, although it was not until the 1880s that he would exhibit his most sketchy works publicly. (Sketches such as the famous paintings of La Grenouillère and the beach at Trouville, now in the National Gallery, London, were almost

certainly intended as private notations rather than as works for public exhibition.) However, his practice of building up a work was to be fairly consistent throughout his life. He would first lay in the main elements of the composition in the appropriate colors in a loose underpainting, and he would then work up all these areas in a range of broad contours and small surface brushstrokes, as fitting to the feature being described. Despite his protestations in later life, this process of elaboration was not always performed in front of the subject, but rather over a period of days or often months in the studio, as Monet's letters of the 1880s to the dealer Durand-Ruel testify.

Many of Monet's views of Paris from the 1860s adopt unusual viewpoints and incorporate ambiguous hints of narratives about the relationships of the tiny figures evoked through his summary brushstrokes. The overall effects of these compositional

Terrace at St Adresse

devices had many precedents, not only the unusual perspectives typical of the Japanese prints of which Monet was an avid collector, but also his awareness of the world of the *flâneur* described with such verve in Charles Baudelaire's *The Painter of Modern Life*. This delightful and influential essay, which nominally describes the achievement of Constantin Guys (1802–92), a draftsman who evocatively captures the fashions and social types of the Second Empire, articulates the unique freedom and anonymity available to the young man as he wanders around absorbing the spectacle of the new Paris. Monet eloquently captures this mood of exploration and mystery in his aloof aerial views of the manicured public gardens, bridges, and boulevards at the heart of Paris and the chance encounters of its suburban fringes.

In 1866, Monet began his response to Manet's scandalous painting *Lunch on the Grass*, which had been rejected by the Salon of 1863 on the grounds of indecency, with a monumental painting of a picnic enjoyed by elegant Parisian men and women. Regrettably, it never came to fruition, and only a sketch and a few fragments survive. Monet did

complete a second large-scale painting of fashionable women at play, *Women in the Garden*, which he executed entirely in the open air. However, it was rejected by the Salon of 1867. This was a period of some personal and professional strain for Monet. His mistress Camille was pregnant with their son Jean and, although Monet's father had been supportive of his son's artistic career, he would not tolerate this romantic alliance.

Portrait of Michel in a Pompom Hat

had also left for London, including, most significantly for Monet, the leading art dealer Paul Durand-Ruel, who soon became a vitally important and lifelong patron for Monet and the Impressionist circle. During the nine months the family spent in London, Monet painted numerous views of the city's parks and of the River Thames. After traveling through Holland in the summer, where he painted at Zaandam near Amsterdam, the Monets returned to France and settled in a suburb to the west of Paris called Argenteuil. Monet remained there until 1878, and many

Suffering financial difficulties, Monet returned to the family home in Le Havre and left Camille in Paris. However, they were reunited after Jean's birth, living first at Etretat and then in Bougival, where Renoir and Pissarro were frequent visitors and colleagues on sketching trips around suburban pleasure spots such as the floating restaurant, La Grenouillère.

In 1870, Monet and Camille were married and made a honeymoon trip to Trouville, a resort on the Normandy coast. With the outbreak of the Franco-Prussian War in July 1870, the Monets took the decision to flee to London. A number of other artistic figures of his friends—Renoir, Sisley, Gustave Caillebotte (1848–94) and Manet—joined him there to paint the life of the River Seine, a site of pleasure boating, swimming, and river cafés as well as a burgeoning industrial town.

Durand-Ruel had been an avid buyer of these paintings, but in 1873 he suffered financial losses. Monet and his friends had to find a new set of patrons, and they embarked on planning an independent exhibition to draw attention to their work. On the boulevard des Capucines in the studio of Nadar, a leading photographer of the day, the Society of Painters, Sculptors and Engravers

held its first exhibition in April of 1874. A contemporary critic coined the term "Impressionism" in response to Monet's unusually sketchy view in grayish-blue and orange of the industrial harbor at Le Havre enshrouded in fog entitled *Impression: Sunrise*. This exhibition achieved a certain notoriety, although it did little to raise the prices that the artists could ask for their works, as proved by the 1875 auction of the Jean-Baptiste Fauré collection of works by Berthe Morisot (1841–95), Renoir, and Sisley. Monet also showed paintings at the second, third, fourth and seventh of the eight exhibitions mounted by the Impressionist group between 1876 and 1884.

Monet met Ernest Hoschedé and his wife Alice in 1876, and they were to play an important role in his later life. Hoschedé commissioned four paintings from Monet to

create a decorative ensemble for the main receiving-room at his home just outside Paris, the Château de Rottembourg at Montgeron. After Hoschedé's bankruptcy and the birth of Monet's second son, Michel, in 1878, the two couples and their eight children decided to form a joint household in Vètheuil. However, Camille, who seemingly had a disease of the womb, died in the fall of the next year. Alice Hoschedé and Monet were to form an open,

rather unconventional relationship that may have contributed to Monet's gradual distancing from his Parisian painter friends and their exhibitions.

Though intimate, the couple lived largely autonomous lives. Although Ernest Hoschedé had created a separate life for himself in the 1880s, Monet and Alice did not marry until after Ernest's death in 1892. After a brief sojourn in Poissy, the family moved to their now-famous house in Giverny. They rented this house until Monet was able to purchase it in 1890, owing to a newfound affluence achieved in a large part by Durand-Ruel's adept and financially rewarding cultivation of American collectors interested in purchasing Monet's works. The family were to spend the rest of their lives at Giverny.

With Alice caring for his children, Monet embarked on a period of frequent painting trips to picturesque corners of France throughout the 1880s. He returned several times to the Normandy and Brittany coasts, as he had always done, but now he chose to paint the more remote sites rather than the tourist-filled resorts. The Parisians at play in Trouville and St Adresse, celebrated in his

Camille Monet, First Wife of the Painter, on her Deathbed

canvases of the 1860s, gave way to the lonely tempest-tossed shores and rock pools of Fécamp and Pourville and the majestic isolation of the hilltop church at Varengeville in 1881 and 1882. He found a favorite motif in the dramatic cliffs and needles of Etretat (a subject made famous a decade before by Gustave Courbet (1819-77)). He returned there in 1883, 1885, and 1886, when he also painted many views of Belle-Ile off the southern coast of Brittany. In 1886, Monet also began to explore more distant regions within France and even the tulip fields of Holland. His lifelong fascination with the cool light and coastal storms of the north was coupled with new explorations of the warm brilliance of the Mediterranean. He visited the south-eastern tip of France, painting

Antibes, View of the Fort

Bordighera, Antibes, and Juan-les-Pins in 1884 and 1889. He also traveled to the Creuse Valley in the heart of France in 1889.

The 1880s and 1890s saw a shift of focus in Monet's life on many levels, in the kind of subject matter he explored, the venues he selected for exhibiting his works, and the huge success and fame that he achieved. Like so many artists and writers at the end of the

nineteenth century, he became dissatisfied with the themes of modernity and urban experience. His art became much more focused on a world of personal sensation before the wonders of nature. A monumental, decorative quality creeps in to his late works. Rather than the external spectacle that delighted Manet and Baudelaire, these paintings offer private spaces of contemplation

which engulf the viewer in their gentle color harmonies and bold compositions. These paintings achieve a world of escape and private reverie which was analogous to the artistic ambitions championed by the Symbolist painters and poets and the Art Nouveau designers.

These new subjects not only widened Monet's own experience and modes of expression but also they attracted keen buyers and dealer-patrons. After the acceptance by the Salon of a painting of an ice floe in 1880, Monet embarked on a new cycle of one-man and group exhibitions with several of the leading private art dealers of the day. In 1883 Monet held a one-man show at the gallery of his old friend and supporter Durand-Ruel. He participated in the group shows organized by Georges Petit in 1885, 1886, and 1887. This relationship with Petit culminated in a retrospective of Monet's work in 1889 which confirmed the popularity and sales of his

The Ice Floes

work. On his return from the trips to Antibes, Monet also exhibited ten paintings with the dealers Boussod and Valadon, which their manager, Theo van Gogh, had purchased. Interestingly, Monet ended this hugely successful exhibition by refusing to accept one of the highest accolades from the French State, the Légion d'Honneur. While he rejected honors for himself, Monet sought a place in the nation's museums for his mentor Manet by orchestrating a campaign of subscriptions

to pay for the purchase of that artist's famously scandalous and innovative depiction of a Parisian courtesan, titled *Olympia*, painted in 1865.

The artistic explorations undertaken on Monet's many painting trips of the 1880s were essentially preliminary work for his great series paintings of the 1890s. In the series, Monet would select a particularly resonant site and subject, such as haystacks, poplar trees on the River Epte, or the façade of Rouen Cathedral, and paint suites of paintings

portraying the motif under various different conditions of light and season. These series lay at the heart of Monet's public exhibiting career in the last decade of the nineteenth century. In a one-man exhibition held in Durand-Ruel's gallery in 1891, Monet included 15 paintings from the haystack series. He also created single-theme exhibitions for subsequent motifs throughout the following years. He showed the poplars at Durand-Ruel's gallery in 1892, the façade of Rouen Cathedral in 1893, the first water-garden series in 1900, the London views in 1904, and a series of 48 water lily paintings, known as "waterscapes," in 1909. The views of Pourville and of early mornings on the River Seine were included in his one-man exhibition at the Georges Petit Gallery in 1898, and the Venice

Poplars on the Bank of the Epte

views were shown at the Bernheim-Jeune Gallery in 1912.

Monet's other great artistic project of the 1890s was the creation of his water garden at Giverny. As soon as he had purchased the house, he began to create an elaborate flower garden incorporating every shade of color and variety of bloom—a palette made of flowers. In 1893, he had the opportunity to buy a second plot of land on the opposite side of the road and railway track that run through the property to this day. Monet elaborated on the indigenous pond and stream by gaining planning permission to alter the flow of water entering the stream and by repeatedly enlarging the pond in 1901 and 1910. Perhaps his most dramatic addition was a bridge, of typical arched Japanese design, which he built

at one end of the pond. This peaceful idyll of his own devising was to be Monet's final subject, which he painted daily for 20 years.

The water lilies paintings led Monet to his last great project: the decorations for the Orangerie. Decorative painting had witnessed an extraordinary revival in the last quarter of the nineteenth century in both official and more esoteric artistic circles. In a speech at the awards banquet for the Salon of 1879, Jules Ferry, Minister of Fine Arts and Education, had called for the decoration of all France's public buildings. Town halls, schools, churches, and museums throughout France were decorated with vast mural schemes

celebrating the Third Republic. This revival of decorative art was paralleled among a set of wealthy patrons who commissioned numerous decorative paintings to ornament the salons of their villas. Similarly, many leading restaurants, such as Maxime's and Le Train Bleu, the latter built at the Gare de Lyon for the World Fair of 1900, sought sympathetic decorative schemes to enhance the Belle Epoque elegance of their dining-rooms. Leading artists from every aesthetic camp of the day were commissioned to create these decorations, from the members of the Nabis group, such as Pierre Bonnard (1867–1947) and Edouard Vuillard

Water Lilies

(1868–1940), to leading Salon painters such as Albert Besnard (1849–1934) and Henri Gervex (1852–1929).

The powerful Republican politician Georges Clemenceau was a close friend and a vociferous champion of Monet's painting. Concerned at his friend's gloom after the death of both his beloved wife Alice in 1910 and his elder son Jean in 1914, Clemenceau cajoled the old painter to embark on a colossal decoration inspired by the water garden. Monet built a special studio in his garden so that he could work in comfort on such monumental canvases. In 1918, he decided to donate the work to the French State. Despite suffering from cataracts in both

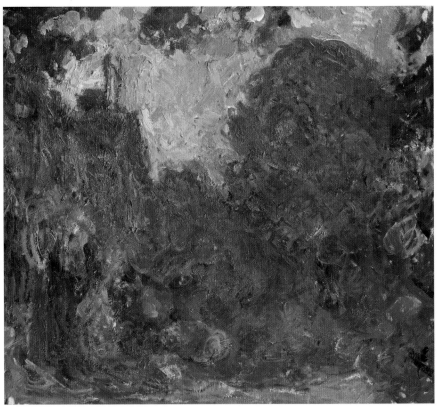

eyes, Monet worked on the project continuously until his death in 1926. Initially, the ensemble was to be housed in a specially built pavilion in the grounds of the Biron Hotel (now the Musée Rodin), but in 1921 it was announced that the murals would be housed in the Orangerie in the Tuilleries Gardens near the Louvre. The architect

Camille Lefèvre designed two oval rooms at ground level to house the paintings, and they were opened to the public on May 16, 1927.

In his long lifetime Monet had started a revolution in art and in thinking about art that has continued to the present day. It involved a new way of looking at art, of daring to paint scenes not previously

considered fit subjects for high art—Monet himself contributed some works that reflected the changing industrial face of the world, including *Unloading Coal* (1875), *Streetside of St Lazare Railway Station* (1877), and *View of Rouen Near the Coast of St Catherine* (c. 1892). When he constructed these paintings he used an uncharacteristically dull and gloomy palette, quite unlike the glowing and subtle colors that were his trademark.

This willingness to investigate the artistic possibilities of subjects that had been regarded as ugly or mundane was a far cry from the earlier focus on what had been previously been regarded as acceptably "picturesque" motifs, beyond which artists ventured at their peril.

Streetside of St Lazare Railway Station

View of Rouen near the Coast of St Catherine

Unlike many artists throughout history and of his own time, Monet was fortunate in that he he lived long enough to enjoy success, both popular and financial. After his early years of struggle, his work was collected by the wealthy and was also bought for public exhibition. The critics who had so disparaged Monet and his "impressionism," had unwittingly, in their attempts to discredit him and his style of painting, contributed to the beginnings of his success and the success of other artists like him, who were beginning to push at the accepted boundaries of art.

Dr Claire O'Mahony

This work is one of the artist's earliest pieces. Claude Monet began his career as a caricaturist, for which he had achieved local success by 1856. The intention behind these cartoons was to emphasize the physical attributes of certain figures, often his class teachers, in a satirical and often unappealing way. In *Bordeaux Wine* Monet achieves this by painting the gentleman's head in complete disproportion, rising out of a wine bottle. His face is almost clown-like, with its rosy cheeks, wide smile, and tufts of fluffy white hair, which are positioned unusually at either side of his forehead. Similar methods were adopted for other caricatures, such as *Dandy with Cigar* (c.1857–58) and *Little Theatrical Group* (c. 1857–60).

By the age of 17, the young artist was already profiting from his work. *Bordeaux Wine* was produced in the same year that Monet's mother died and close to the time between 1855 and 1857 when he left school to pursue his ambition of becoming a painter. His skillful and satirical caricatures were displayed in the window of a local framer, where they drew crowds of appreciative viewers. It was this early success as a caricaturist that delayed Monet's pursuit of a career as a landscape artist.

A CORNER OF THE
ARTIST'S STUDIO
1861

MUSEE D'ORSAY, PARIS.
CELIMAGE.SA/LESSING ARCHIVE

➡ In 1861, Monet's time at the Académie Suisse was terminated by his call-up for military service. He entered the cavalry regiment and was posted to Algeria. In the same year he produced *A Corner of the Artist's Studio*.

This painting provides an intricate and intimate insight into a part of the artist's personal life. This is one of Monet's early paintings, which, again, adopts a more conservative attitude in terms of its palette and content. This painting is a very traditional study of a respectable gentleman, with books, guns, and fine art suggesting learning and an elevated social status. Very different from his early caricatures and later waterscapes, this piece seems more realistic than impressionistic, as Monet once again stays within an accepted and respected artistic framework. There is close attention to detail, as illustrated by the careful execution of the rug and wallpaper. Even the pages of the books are creased to suggest that they have been read. There is a very authentic feel to this piece, which has the intrinsic beauty of so many of Monet's works.

STILL LIFE:
PIECE OF BEEF
1864
MUSEE D'ORSAY, PARIS.
CELIMAGE.SA/SCALA ARCHIVES

◄ *Piece of Beef* seems almost out of context as an artwork produced by Claude
Monet. However, it is important that we view this piece as one of the artist's early
attempts to seek recognition for his talent. This still life, like others produced by
Monet in the early 1860s, is truly conformist in terms of its form and content.
This was solely to please the art establishment and gain success through a more
traditional approach.

Artistically, however, there are also some interesting aspects to this piece.
The deep contrast of the red raw meat set against the depths of a black backdrop
provides a powerful image, even though the palette is limited to these two main
colors. There is a stark quality to this painting and an obvious detail and skill in
its execution. A similar effect is achieved in Monet's still life *The Hunting Trophy*
(1862), in which there is an elaborate composition and detailed treatment of the
subject matter.

Although the still life paintings were fewer in number, these two early works
show the artist's growing ability and confidence as a painter. The quality of their
finish proves how determined Monet was to understand the fundamental principles
of good art, through traditional training.

THE GREEN WAVE
1865

⬆ This canvas is swept with a deep green wave and we are launched right into its path. Monet draws us close to a boat that is wrestling with the rise of the water. In the near and far distance, gray sails indicate where other vessels are passing.

The Green Wave is stylistically very different from Monet's other river paintings from the 1870s, such as *Pleasure Boats* (1872) (see page 68) and *Fishing Boat at Anchor, Rouen* (1872), where the boats are distanced into their backgrounds and a clear perspective is drawn between the horizon and the sea. The water is also painted with an eerie realism, whereas in *The Green Wave* the wave is a less detailed mass of color, fringed by seams of bright white, to represent the resistance of the water against the boat. These areas of white really enhance the painting, as the rest of the scene is distilled by a layer of gray to give the impression of a looming storm.

In *The Green Wave*, Monet demonstrates the theory that light can be likened to a wave constituted from broad swatches of various shades of green. The bright green used here is different from the blues and grays found in his other works.

In 1865, Monet successfully exhibited two paintings, including this one, at the Salon in Paris for the first time. This was an important breakthrough in his career. One of the pictures exhibited was a marine scene painted at Honfleur.

The Cart, Route through the Snow at Honfleur shows the town as seen from the approach road. It is a winter's day, but the painting is not dark and gloomy as Monet's snowscapes often are. Instead there is a light in the sky that seems to be generated by the sun, which is not yet visible. The white of the snow is not diluted by too much darkness from the buildings or the cart. The overall effect of the painting is quite bright.

Although this is an early work, some elements of Monet's later technique are clearly evident within it. There is some short brushwork, using contrasting shades of white, on the snow on the road. Monet is also conscious of the parallel lines formed by the cartwheels in the snow and the ditch by the side of the road. This use of lines and shapes in the landscape would become very important in his later work.

THE CART, ROUTE
THROUGH THE SNOW
AT HONFLEUR

1865

MUSEE DU LOUVRE, PARIS.
CELIMAGE.SA/LESSING ARCHIVE

This is a portrait of Victor Jacquemont, a watercolorist and engraver who worked for several newspapers at the time. However, the picture has been repeatedly cataloged with varying titles and it is difficult to confirm which is the correct one, leading it to be known simply as *Portrait of a Man*.

Manet's influence can be seen in the picture, as it can in other works by Monet from this period; the lack of detailed shading on the figure means he has been painted with solid contrasting colors. Working up the body, Monet starts with white only for the shoes. He then switches to gray for the pants, with only a little shading around the knees and ankles, brown for the jacket and vest, and flesh for the face. The colors are not varied in tone, so that the figure seems very flat on the canvas. The effect of sunlight or the shadow from the umbrella is not painted in.

A similar technique was used in *Camille on the Beach* (1870–71) (see page 64). However, in the latter, Monet has taken it to its logical conclusion. The brushstrokes have become thicker and the paint is laid on heavily. He concentrates purely on color, so that Camille's face does not have any features. The sky is one solid color, and even the sea has little variety.

PORTRAIT OF A MAN
1865
KUNSTHAUS, ZURICH.
CELIMAGE.SA/LESSING ARCHIVE

The subject matter of this painting is not controversial, but Monet's treatment of it is. Monet started work on this massive canvas with the intention of submitting it to the Salon exhibition of 1866 and causing a sensation. The sheer scale of the work meant it was not ready in time, and Monet abandoned it.

The unfinished canvas reveals a conventional scene of picnickers in the forest. However, Monet is attempting to treat the people as a natural part of the landscape. There is no storyline to the painting, and this is emphasized by the uncentered composition: the eye is not drawn to any one point, and the people are simply a part of their surroundings. Monet wanted to create a sense of spontaneity with this painting, as if it were the capturing of a moment. This is underlined by the casual actions of the figures. One woman is caught in the act of touching her hair; another is about to put down a plate. This realism was very unusual in art of this period. Manet's influence is felt in the painting, but Monet hoped to avoid the moral judgment that Manet suffered with *Olympia* by not using controversial subject matter such as nude figures.

LUNCH ON THE GRASS
1865
PUSHKIN MUSEUM, MOSCOW.
CELIMAGE.SA/SCALA ARCHIVES

THE PATH AT CHAILLY,
FONTAINEBLEAU FOREST
1865
MUSEE D'ORSAY, PARIS.
CELIMAGE.SA/LESSING ARCHIVE

➡ This painting is rich in color and detail. We are positioned at ground level in front of the leaves, with trees nearby and in the distance, where they reach far beyond the height of the canvas. Monet shows another deserted scene and the track running along the ground adds to this effect. There is no sign of animal life, which seems quite odd in a painting of a forest.

The leaves on the forest floor are painted in concentrated detail. A few of them are dotted with white specks so that they glisten in the sunlight. Set in contrast to their darker partners lying nearby, it looks as though they are dancing lightly across the ground.

The trunk of the tree to the near right of the canvas has also been executed with thought and time. Where the bark has been breached or has rotted, Monet has used a darker color.

On the trees themselves, he has used the paintbrush to repeat a lighter color throughout the mass of leaves, so that we can see a flicker of light running through the canopy. The whole piece seems to represent a scene from early morning.

In the distance, the foliage running toward the left of the canvas progressively loses its detail and color until it forms a thick dark block of brown-green that disappears into the horizon. This gives a wonderful perspective, added to by the bleakness of the sky, its tone unvarying throughout.

Claude Monet

Women in the Garden

WOMEN IN THE GARDEN

1866

MUSEE D'ORSAY, PARIS.

CELIMAGE.SA/LESSING ARCHIVE

◁ Camille Doncieux posed for all four women in this painting, wearing hired dresses: the impoverished Monet could not afford clothes like these. Monet submitted the painting, which was painted at Ville d'Avray, for the 1867 Salon, but it was rejected. Artists such as Daumier and Manet also criticized the picture.

Monet was aiming to make two significant points with *Women in the Garden*. This large size of canvas was traditionally reserved for historical or religious paintings that carried a moral message for the viewer. By painting an unremarkable modern scene, Monet was declaring that these everyday moments, painted in a realistic manner, were just as important in the art world as esteemed historical or religious subjects.

His second point was concerned with the spontaneity of art and painting exactly what was in front of the artist. Instead of sketching the scene and then completing it in a studio, Monet painted the entire work in the open air. This became known as *plein-air* technique. So determined was he to make this painting seem real that he dug a trench in the garden in order to have the canvas at the right level while he worked on it.

JEANNE-MARGUERITE,
THE IMAGE IN
THE GARDEN

1866

THE HERMITAGE, ST PETERSBURG.
CELIMAGE.SA/SCALA ARCHIVES

⬅ Another work that was inspired by Manet's artistic style, *Jeanne-Marguerite, the Image in the Garden* completes the isolation of the individual that Monet had attempted to capture in *Women in the Garden* (1866) (see page 42). In the slightly earlier work, although the women form a group, they seem removed from each other. Here Monet finalizes that isolation by having a lone female in the garden.

Her isolation is further completed by placing her to the far left edge of the canvas, so she is removed from the main focus of the picture. This gives an unsettled feel to the composition, which is similar to that achieved in the earlier work. In *Women in the Garden* three of the women are placed left of center, and the eye struggles to find a main focal point between them. This is achieved in *Jeanne-Marguerite, the Image in the Garden* by patches of color. The viewer is drawn repeatedly from the yellow to the red flowers and then across to the white dress.

The technique of using blocks of colors, employed in *Women in the Garden,* is repeated here with more vigor. The sky is almost a solid patch of blue, the dress a block of white, and the grass a strip of green. This gives a flat effect to the picture.

CAMILLE WITH
A LITTLE DOG
1866
PRIVATE COLLECTION, ZURICH.
CELIMAGE.SA/LESSING ARCHIVE

◄ This intimate portrait is one of the few that shows Camille in a formal pose. Although not shown face on, her features have been recorded in the kind of detail lacking in many of the paintings she posed for.

The difference in Monet's attitude to Camille in this painting and in a later one, *The Reader* (1872), is interesting. In *Camille with a Little Dog* his aim is to create a portrait of Camille: there is no vivid background to distract the eye and she is definitely the center of attention. Her profile is emphasized by being painted against a dark color. The quick brushstrokes representing the shaggy dog contrast with the careful work on Camille's face and underline that Monet was trying to make Camille the only subject of interest. This is not the case with *The Reader*, where the background, and even Camille's dress, are perhaps more important than who she is. She is painted as part of the scenery, almost an incidental feature of the landscape.

By posing Camille for *The Reader* with her face turned down toward her book, her features are not easily distinguishable. In *Camille with a Little Dog*, she looks steadily forward, and some sense of her character can be gleaned from the attitude of her head and her quiet pose.

FISHING BOATS,
HONFLEUR
1866

MUZEUL NATIONAL DE ARTA,
BUCHAREST.
CELIMAGE.SA/LESSING ARCHIVE

➡ What is instantly striking about this painting is the unusual and bold use of color. Instead of using his traditional small, hasty brushstrokes, Monet has applied the paint thickly, creating solid areas of color on the boats, allowing them to leap from the painting and to our attention. At the same time there is an overall sense of stillness. Even the reflections of the boat hulls in the water do not create any ripples, giving the impression that they are resting on land rather than on liquid.

The colors used for the vessels—green, white, red, orange, and black—recall the Fauves. The Fauvist André Derain (1880-1954) is renowned for the bright, bold strokes of color that he used to create vivid and exciting images.

Surrounding the blocks of color on the four boats, a murky, quite diluted brown represents the water, and a darker brown, enhanced with even darker streaks, details the sails. The whole composition is set against a white background, which is also bold in its application. This is a very unusual piece for Monet to have produced.

Artistically, *Fishing Boats, Honfleur* does not employ the deeply impressionistic style found in Monet's garden works and some of his other boat and water paintings. In, for example, *Pleasure Boats* (1872) (see page 68), the vessels float away from the viewer—our focus is more on the water itself, and its realism. In *Fishing Boats, Honfleur*, their striking masses of color force us to confront the boats. This work shows Monet's versatility and dexterity as an artist, always seeking innovation through variations in technique, style, and medium.

ICE FLOES ON THE
SEINE AT BOUGIVAL
1867

MUSEE D'ORSAY, PARIS.
CELIMAGE.SA/LESSING ARCHIVE

◧ The composition of this painting, and its date, suggest that Monet was still interested in the same techniques that he had been using while in Normandy. Three years earlier, he had been engrossed in painting snow scenes, but not in the same style as this.

The painting is almost monochromatic in color scheme with little variation from the gray and white of the palette. This seems suitable for recording a dull winter's day. It is in contrast to his later treatment of the Seine in winter, where the color scheme is more varied, and the touches of yellow and light blue help to give the picture a warmer tone. In addition, his use of color and brushstroke is preoccupied with laying on small brushstrokes of individual colors to create an all-encompassing atmosphere. In *Ice Floes on the Seine at Bougival*, the technique is more concerned with toning in brushstrokes to create a solid block of color.

The trees to the left are painted as vertical lines that form a screen that is reflected in the water. This is reminiscent of contemporary Japanese art. The use of color and the decorative and simplistic interpretation of the landscape are all in keeping with Japanese art, which was very popular at this time.

LANDSCAPE AROUND HONFLEUR IN SNOW

1867

MUSEE DU LOUVRE, PARIS.
CELIMAGE.SA/LESSING ARCHIVE

◄ Snow was an interesting subject for the Impressionist painters, because of the effects it created with light and because of the way it altered the shape of the landscape. In *Landscape around Honfleur in Snow*, Monet demonstrates his particular interest in the effects of changing light on a scene. He maintains his approach of contrasting the white of the snow with darker patches, usually in the form of debris or in the branches of trees. Then, surrounding these patches, in the distant horizon, is a darker shadow, silhouetting a line of larger trees that threaten the landscape.

This was Monet's approach in his snowscapes from the 1860s and 1870s, although we can see a stark contrast in his use of color here and in *Norway, the Red Houses at Bjornegaard* (1895) (see page 198). In this latter piece, the white emphasizes the red of the buildings and the blue of the sky.

The effect of Monet's treatment of color in *Landscape around Honfleur in Snow* is one of somber bleakness, largely abandoned in his waterscapes of Giverny. The dark gray sky gives an indication of time of day, perhaps early evening. The application of the medium is fairly hasty.

Claude Monet

TERRACE AT
ST ADRESSE
1867

M.O.M.A., NEW YORK.
CELIMAGE.SA/EDIMEDIA

⬆ Poverty forced Monet to return to the family home around 1867, and while there he painted this view from one of the upstairs rooms. The seated man is Monet's father. Monet's stepson commented later that the abundance of flowers on the terrace suggests that Monet's love of flowers was inherited from his parents. The painting appears composed and almost artificial when compared with some of the earlier works, which are deliberately given a more spontaneous feel.

Monet later referred to this painting as the "Chinese painting with flags." At that time the words "Japanese" and "Chinese" were often interchanged. He owned some Japanese prints, and their influence is seen in this work. The flags that dominate the picture dissect the three horizontal bands of the painting—the terrace, the sea, and the sky—providing a vertical balance.

The composition itself is unconventional, with the faces of the people turned away from the viewer. The boats and ships in the background emphasise the modernity of the scene, as they were vital to trade in the town. Their shapes on the horizon are sharply geometric, contributing to the oriental tone of the painting. While Monet's treatment of the sky is flat, the sea shows signs of his fascination with its every changing color, a fascination that emerges strongly in later works.

THE BEACH
AT ST ADRESSE
1867

THE CHICAGO ART INSTITUTE,
CHICAGO.
CELIMAGE.SA/LESSING ARCHIVE

➡ This picture is unique to Monet in so many ways. Firstly, we are drawn directly onto the beach to view the scene, whereas Monet usually positions himself at a height before painting. What is even more noticeable is the appearance of people almost directly in front of the viewer, whereas traditionally in Monet's paintings, the people are totally featureless, mere silhouettes of color across the setting. Another novel aspect is the attention to detail. Pebbles appear in the sand, and the color of the water and sand vary according to their depth. The boats are also more detailed, as are the buildings in the distance, and the clouds are very realistic.

One of the comfortable features of this painting is its arrangement. Although the canvas seems to be bustling with activity, with the many vessels littered around the scene, and the interaction between the three men standing by a boat on the shore, compositionally, the placement of everything in the painting is reminiscent of Monet's beach series. The cliffs hang to the left of the canvas, and we view the scene from the right of the beach, as in *Fishing Boats in Front of the Beach and the Cliffs of Pourville* (1882) (see page 138) and *the Beach at Pourville, Sunset* (1882).

JEAN MONET, SLEEPING
1868

NY-CARLSBERG-GLYPTOTHEK,
COPENHAGEN.
CELIMAGE.SA/LESSING ARCHIVE

➡ This is a very loving, thoughtful portrait of Monet's son, Jean Monet, completed in 1868, when the child was two years old. Jean often appeared in Monet's landscape paintings, sometimes with Camille and at other times on his own. However, in all of those works he is identifiable only as a small youth, rather than an individual in his own right.

This is quite an intimate portrait, accomplished with a fine detail and use of medium. The palette is soft and considerate toward the subject. The pale whites and blues, grays, and pinks are softened to suggest the features of his face. Monet depicts Jean resting peacefully in his sleep.

However, in *Jean Monet Sleeping* we can identify a development in the style of the artist. By this time, Monet had become quite comfortable with using thicker brushstrokes and blocks of color to constitute solid areas on a canvas. We can see this particularly on Jean's face, as the thick skin-colored brushstrokes are confidently shaped to suit its curvature.

Monet pays minimal attention to the detail of Jean's attire, unlike in some of his other portraits, such as *The Japanese Woman* (1875) (see page 98). However, this lack of commitment to detail was consistent with his recordings of Michel Monet and some of his paintings of Camille. Instead, there is a certain sweetness in the way in which Monet portrays his family.

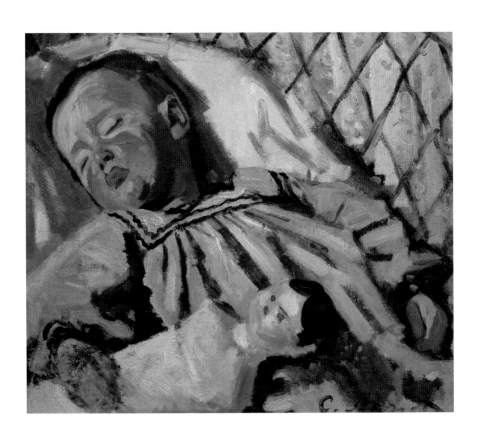

HOTEL DES ROCHES
NOIRES, TROUVILLE
1870

MUSEE D'ORSAY, PARIS.
CELIMAGE.SA/LESSING ARCHIVE

◀ In this painting, as well as in others depicting Trouville, Monet seeks to
perpetuate the concept of *plein air*. The cursory presentation of the figures and the
hasty application of the medium serve to establish these paintings as works of
spontaneity. This was the intention with most, if not all of Monet's impressionistic
paintings, since their purpose was to capture a fleeting moment in time, as a camera
would, and store it on the canvas. Monet would loosely record the fundamental
aspects of a scene, such as the light in the sky, the reflection on the water, and the
movement of the people. He would finish with a series of short, rapid brushstrokes
and contrasts of color and shade, in what became known as the Impressionist way.

In *Hôtel des Roches Noires, Trouville* Monet successfully captures a lively and
luminous quality. A dancing flag peers from the top end of the canvas, and the sun's
brightness is captured in the whiteness of the people's dress and the shadows cast
in the shade. Clouds appear as wisps of white in the sky. Although the painting
creates a sense of solidarity for the onlookers as they face the crowd of people, they
are partially removed from the main action.

ON THE BEACH AT
TROUVILLE
1870–71

MUSEE MARMOTTAN, PARIS.
CELIMAGE.SA/LESSING ARCHIVE

◧ Painted while on holiday with Boudin, this picture depicts Camille and Boudin's wife on the beach at the popular French tourist spot of Trouville. Monet's choice of subject again reflects his desire to record modern scenes. He chose to show this familiar resort in an untraditional way.

The viewer is thrust in very close to the two women. This is the opposite technique to that used in another work from this location, *The Beach at Trouville* (1870). The result is to make the viewer slightly uncomfortable, as if he were invading an intimate scene. This discomfort is furthered by the relationship between the two women. The central space between them is empty; neither woman acknowledges the presence of the other. Their features are not detailed, so there is an air of anonymity about them. Similarly, the people walking in *The Beach at Trouville* are not painted in detail.

In the background of this painting other tourists can be seen, also devoid of identifiable features. This lack of detail, combined with the quick, heavy brushstrokes, adds to the spontaneity of the painting. In both works Monet is advocating the *plein-air* technique.

CAMILLE ON THE BEACH
1870–71

MUSEE MARMOTTAN, PARIS.
CELIMAGE.SA/LESSING ARCHIVE

➡ The treatment of the subject in this painting is simplistic. The figure poses on the beach facing toward the viewer and in close proximity, yet she has no features to her face, with the merest hint of an outline for her nose and eyes. She is an anonymous woman without identity.

Monet's formal portrait *Camille with a Little Dog* (1866) (see page 46) is in stark contrast to this work. It depicts Camille in profile but with careful attention paid to her features, so that her face is revealed in detail. Her clothes are treated to the same level of care, and she would be recognizable as the subject in reality. Part of Camille's lack of detail in *Camille on the Beach* may be due to the unfinished nature of the work—in places the canvas shows through. While this alone does not necessarily indicate that a work is unfinished, the lack of a signature adds weight to the assumption. Monet did not sign all his finished work, but in this case it seems certain he had not finished the painting.

The brushstrokes are laid on thickly and are clearly visible to the viewer. The work has an air of spontaneity that is especially evident when examining the sea, which is painted in with a few brushstrokes using only three colors.

TRAIN IN THE COUNTRYSIDE

1870–71

⬆ In the 1870s, Monet produced several works featuring a railway bridge and train, especially during his visits to Argenteuil. Often the train would be quite insignificant, the only recognition of its existence the billowing smoke.

In *Train in the Countryside* there is an even greater focus on the countryside and the people in the foreground. Most of the train itself is hidden by the treetops and the smoke exhaled from its engine is mostly camouflaged by the clouds in the sky. Both the carriages and the people in them are painted in black, almost as silhouettes against the brightness of the sky.

A compositional and tonal balance is achieved in this work, with the horizon clearly defined and the brilliant white of the people's clothing being reflected in the clouds and pale sky. The brightness of the green used to represent the grass shows the position of the sun, which is contrasted with the darker areas of shadow surrounding the bigger trees, as well as the shadowy carriages of the distant train.

There is also a variation in brushstroke and color application. The leaves on the trees and the dresses of the people are executed using shorter and more frequently applied dots of paint, whereas the field in the foreground is a solid green.

⬆ One of the more subtle and interesting aspects of *Windmill at Zaandam* are the birds in the sky. They are an unusual ingredient in Monet's work, since we usually find that the sky is unencumbered by objects, apart from the occasional cloud. In *Windmill at Zaandam* the sky is bleak, with small washes of gray representing clouds, as its tone is mirrored in the water.

Although *Windmill at Zaandam* does feature people, they are not the focal point of the entire piece and, traditionally for Monet, the colors chosen to depict the figures are reflected in scenes of the background. The main focus of our attention becomes the windmill on the bank to the left of the canvas.

The painting itself is primarily composed of three colors—green, red, and black—all strong, emotive shades. As viewers, we are positioned at the level of the water, so that the windmill towers above us. The shooting green reeds are also quite potent, since Monet uses firm and solid streaks of color to define their position. Their reflection creates quite a vivid response, especially when set against the gray of the water.

WINDMILL AT
ZAANDAM
1871
NY-CARLSBERG-GLYPTOTHEK,
COPENHAGEN.
CELIMAGE.SA/LESSING ARCHIVE

PLEASURE BOATS
1872

MUSEE D'ORSAY, PARIS.
CELIMAGE.SA/EDIMEDIA

Boating as a hobby and pastime became very popular in France in the nineteenth century. At the time many people worked long days in the city, choosing the weekends to visit either the country or seaside, where many went aboard the pleasure boats.

For Monet, his boating scenes represented the attempts by a typical Frenchman to enter into a dialogue with nature. For this reason the paintings are frequently empty of people and seem very isolated moments. In this picture there are only a couple of people on the bank, and their features are indecipherable. In *Fishing Boat at Anchor* (1872) there is only one man on board, and his isolation is exaggerated by the size of the boat. Both paintings devote a lot of space to the sky, which adds to the insignificance of the individuals.

Prior to his move to Argenteuil, Monet painted only merchant ships and working boats. *Fishing Boat at Anchor* shows such a boat. Once at Argenteuil, however, Monet rarely produced marine paintings that did not feature pleasure craft, and *Pleasure Boats* is typical of those he painted at the time.

ARGENTEUIL
1872
CELIMAGE.SA/EDIMEDIA

← *Argenteuil* is a light and airy piece, which has been beautifully crafted with a combination of complex fine lines and a cool, blended palette. Compared with some of his earlier, somewhat dramatic scenes, which were painted on a dark red-brown surface, in *Argenteuil* Monet used unmixed paints, applied directly onto a canvas that had been prepared with a pure white undercoat. This served to enhance the luminosity of each color in the painting. The sail of the boat and the white buildings in the distance are a brilliant white.

Monet depicts a peaceful and tranquil setting, showing two men working on the boats along the river, with the fine lines providing the minimal definition in this painting. Some attention has been given to the white buildings in the distance, the windows of which have been detailed with fine black lines. However, the features of the men cannot be deciphered, and the detail of the landscaped horizon is lost in small wisps of color.

ARGENTEUIL RAILWAY STATION

1872

CONSEIL GENERAL DU VAL D'OISE,
CERGY-PONTOISE.
CELIMAGE.SA/LESSING ARCHIVE

➜ Argenteuil became the familiar and favored location for Monet's series of paintings of the railway station and the railway bridge. This painting seems to combine its primary function as an Impressionist painting with some rather more unusual effects. The blocks of heavy paint are not usually associated with the works of Claude Monet. Here, he makes use of a primarily gray palette in a novel and expressive way. His use of color provides an interesting effect, as our view of the train and the station is distorted by the blending of grays. This is compensated for by the restricted use of a red-brown color to define the station building. Further patches of blue peep through the masses of gray and gray-white clouds. The differing shades of gray provide the mere suggestion of a horizon.

There is still an element of detail, although this is really confined to the train itself. Apart from this, the impressionistic aspect of the work becomes more obvious, since Monet is not intent on a providing a detailed portrayal of the figures and distant buildings. These are simply constructed through a series of agitated outlines.

Overall, Monet displays a familiar scene in a novel and interesting way, through an unexpected combination of color and artistic style.

STILL LIFE WITH
MELON
1872

◄ Monet painted very few still lifes. This study of fruit is treated in a similar manner to his landscape paintings, in the sense that the composition is structured around parallel planes. *Still Life with Melon* is not treated with the obvious banding approach evident in some of Monet's landscapes, although this compositional technique is present. The wall in the background forms one strip of color; the tablecloth creates another square of color that is prevented from reaching completely across the canvas by the strip of dark tabletop on the left-hand side of the picture. These lines of varying color create strong geometric shapes on the canvas. It is easy to see a triangle in the right-hand corner where the wood meets the tablecloth and the frame. Similarly, the wall forms a rectangle.

These geometric shapes are disrupted by the fruit and plates used as the focal points of the composition. It is not by accident that Monet chose round fruits as his subject: the roundness of the melon, grapes, peaches, and the plate contrast with the geometric shapes of their background. The treatment of varying color and light on these draws the eye away from the solid colors with which the backdrops have been painted in. As a result, the whole is harmonized.

CAMILLE MONET,
THE PAINTER'S FIRST
WIFE (1847–79)
1872

MUSEE MARMOTTAN, PARIS.
CELIMAGE.SA/LESSING ARCHIVE

➔ This is one of several intimate portraits of his wife Camille that Monet completed during the 1870s. However, this painting is particularly sensitive and emotive, with its vibrant use of a cool palette, reminiscent of the painter's earlier, darker works.

This piece seems to tell a narrative through its delicate execution, as Monet becomes preoccupied with catching the effect of light on a canvas and capturing a natural, free expression on Camille's face. Here, the darker, misty browns of the background contrast with the bright blues and whites of her dress and skin. Her dark hair and eyes provide a striking focal point.

We can draw several points of comparison and similarity between this and other portraits produced by the artist. Unlike other depictions of his wife, such as *Camille on the Beach* (1870-71) (see page 64), where he deliberately caught and painted the subject unawares, in *Camille Monet* there is a more intimate expression, and an engagement between the observer and subject. Although Camille seems quite aloof, her expression is somewhat distressed or worried. Although she does not directly involve herself with us, we are drawn to her through our concern for her.

THE ZUIDERKERK
AT AMSTERDAM

1872

PHILADELPHIA MUSEUM OF ART,
PHILADELPHIA.
CELIMAGE.SA/EDIMEDIA

◁ There is some confusion about the date of this painting. Monet visited Holland in the summer of 1871, yet this painting is dated 1872. It is now generally agreed that, despite the date, this and another painting, also dated 1872, are actually part of the 1871 series.

The composition of this painting is centered on the spire, with the canal leading up to it. On the right are the tall buildings of Amsterdam, with people moving along the pavement and over the bridge. These people are painted as flecks. The reflections of the buildings in the water are represented by yellow brushstrokes only, with no detail to them. This is the same as in The *Parliament at Sunset* (1904), where the buildings' reflection is identified only as a dark patch on the water.

A comparison of these two paintings reveals that by 1904 Monet was less concerned about observing the boundaries between buildings and water. In *The Parliament at Sunset* it is difficult to identify where the building ends and the reflection begins. In *The Zuiderkerk at Amsterdam* the water is clearly separated from the buildings and there is no danger of buildings and reflection merging. The painting is in focus and uses strong blocks of color, whereas the London painting has a mist over it that prevents a detailed look at the subject.

IMPRESSION: SUNRISE
1872

MUSEE MARMOTTAN, PARIS.
CELIMAGE.SA/LESSING ARCHIVE

⬆ This painting was included in the first exhibition held in 1874 by the Society of Painters, Sculptors, and Engravers, of which Monet was a founder member.

A critic who attended the exhibition, Louis Leroy, wrote an article in *Le Charivari* in which he used the term "Impressionist," based on the title of this painting. Despite the fact that Leroy had used the word derisively, the group decided to adopt it. Impressionist art is concerned with capturing on canvas the light and color of a fleeting moment, usually with brilliant colors painted in small strokes, side by side, rather than blended together.

Ironically, *Impression: Sunrise* is not typical of Monet's work, although it does carry elements of his normal style. The horizon has disappeared and the water, sky, and reflections have all merged together. The buildings and ships in the background are vague shapes and the red sun dominates the painting.

⬆ In this painting Monet has restricted himself to the essentials only, his aim being to create an overall impression. For this reason there is no detail on the sea or the shore but merely strokes of color. The landscape of *The Cliffs at St Adresse* is relatively calm.

The horseshoe of land provides a balanced curve. The curves and rounded ends to the cliffs give the whole picture a soft, undramatic feel. *The Cliffs at St Adresse* has a wash of yellow that encompasses the land and the beach, creating a warm glow that is reflected in the sky.

The paintings Monet produced of the Normandy coast were exhibited in 1898 and proved very popular with the buying public. The combination of familiar scenes and aesthetic presentation meant that these pictures sold easily.

THE CLIFFS AT
ST ADRESSE
1873
COURTESY OF EDIMEDIA

Boulevard des Capucines

BOULEVARD DES
CAPUCINES

1873

NESLON-ATKINS MUSEUM OF ART,
KANSAS CITY.
CELIMAGE.SA/LESSING ARCHIVE

◄ Depicting a modern scene, Monet shows a Paris that is bustling and full of action. He has caught the fleeting nature of movement precisely by dabbing on paint to represent people, rather than dwelling on their detail. This technique is also used in *The Beach at Trouville* (1870) where the people are equally lacking in detail. He also picks another modern subject—the tourist resort.

As well as creating a spontaneous painting that dwells on the instantaneousness of the moment, Monet is also investigating the effects of winter light in *Boulevard des Capucines*. This is the cause of the off-white glow in the sky which reflects onto the street below. Against this, the people seem like dark marks, and this earned them the description of "black tongue-lickings" from the critic Leroy. The different effects of sunlight would especially be understood by the contemporary viewer since the work was displayed with a companion piece depicting the street in summer.

In *The Beach at Trouville*, Monet paints on a level with his subject, so that everything is seen to scale and the numbers of people are camouflaged. In *Boulevard des Capucines* his view is from above, looking down. This increases the impression of the people as a small, scurrying crowd in a city of wide boulevards and tall, modern buildings.

⬆ This scene from nature contrasts with the recent paintings that Monet had been doing, which were mainly of city subjects. Its soft tranquillity reflects some of the warmth of a summer's day: the figures merge with their surroundings, almost melting into them; the boy at the front of the painting has a body that disappears into the grass, and the dress of the woman matches some of the darker shades of grass on the right.

Figures that fade into a rural background are entirely appropriate to Monet's views on nature. He felt that nature was not there to serve man but that man was a part of nature. Hence, the figures in this painting are not the main focus. If it were not for the sloping edge of the poppies drawing the eye of the viewer back from the first group of people to the second on the horizon, the figures could be overlooked. The dominant force of this painting is without doubt the poppies.

Painted in an almost abstract style, the splashes of red draw the observer's eye at once, despite the fact that roughly half the canvas is given over to sky, creating a feeling of an airy summer's day. The blue of the sky contrasts with the red of the poppies and ensures that the landscape, as opposed to the people, leaves the strongest impression on the viewer.

➡ Although not as controversial as the artist's *Lunch on the Grass* (1865) (see page 37), this painting works in a similar way. In neither piece is there a central focus to which our attention is drawn. Instead, the human figures become an integral part of their natural surroundings. The two women are mostly hidden by the hanging branches of a tree and, especially with the lady in yellow, little flashes of color matching her dress are dotted around the tree, camouflaging her further into its form. This is a familiar technique used by Monet to incorporate all of the elements of his painting.

This is one of Monet's most famous works, demonstrating a refined impressionistic technique. *Lunch* is aesthetically endearing, and yet Monet is principally using his canvas to capture a single moment in time, just before the two ladies sit to lunch. There is a certain naivety about this piece, and we feel uninvolved in what is going on. Yet, on the other hand, we feel intrigued by the plethora of colors that Monet has employed in this work.

WOMAN SEATED ON
A BENCH
1874

TATE GALLERY, LONDON.
CELIMAGE.SA/LESSING ARCHIVE

➡ This woman forms a striking presence on the canvas. Instead of being in harmony with her surroundings, Monet places her against a backdrop of a green bench and green trees. Her dress of pink and white makes a strong shape in contrast with this. She is deliberately placed out of harmony with her surroundings, and this gives her a commanding presence.

Her parasol, hat, and dress define her as a fashionable woman. Monet uses these to form shapes and solid lines that are geometric in design. Little effort is made to shade her dress or to make use of any shadowing in the painting. The strong, solid shape of the woman is balanced by regular horizontal lines on the bench and vertical lines representing the foliage behind. This style has often been compared to Manet's.

The bench itself is flat and, were it not for the woman seated on it, it would appear as a screen of green rather than having any depth to it. Perspective and depth are not of importance in this painting. Monet is primarily concerned with creating an overall impression using strong shapes and lines.

THE RAILWAY BRIDGE,
ARGENTEUIL
1874

MUSEE D'ORSAY, PARIS.
CELIMAGE.SA/LESSING ARCHIVE

➡ Monet was fascinated with painting this railway bridge during the time he spent
at Argenteuil. For him it represented the coming together of modernity and nature.
He always painted it with a train rushing across and sending out clouds of smoke.
This explosion of energy was contrasted with the tranquillity of the water. The bridge,
which has contact with both, links the two different worlds.

This is in contrast to *Unloading Coal* (1875) (see page 96), where the bridge
appears to be a barrier separating the workers from the passers-by. The solid paint
on the bridge in the *The Railway Bridge, Argenteuil* is contrasted with the colors
used on the water. In places the brushwork is applied sketchily. However, Monet uses
denser and more detailed strokes to illustrate the movement of light over the water.
This is especially evident on the water moving under the bridge.

Unloading Coal has dark colors used repeatedly to give the whole painting a
gloomy appearance. This painting does not have one dominant color or tone;
instead each section is given a color of its own that complements its neighbor and
also separates it: for example, the greeny yellow of the grass is not related to the
gray of the bridge, but the tones manage to complement one another.

THE BRIDGE AT
ARGENTEUIL
1874

MUSEE D'ORSAY, PARIS.
CELIMAGE.SA/EDIMEDIA

◁ A number of paintings from Argenteuil depict boats and this is a classic example.
Monet had a very commercial mind and, since boating was a popular pastime for
Parisians in the 1890s, his choice of subject matter was guaranteed to appeal to the
buying public. The whole is a tranquil scene that has a translucent air to it.

The colors harmonize together to help create an aesthetic view. Broken color is
used where it is necessary to depict the surface of the water affected by light, and
under the arches of the bridge where the light reflects off the water. By using
adjacent lines, an almost translucent effect is created. The bridge to the right is
another feature that Monet favored in paintings at this time. In this picture the lines
and arches provide a geometric balance to the translucence of the water.

Unloading Coal (1875) (see page 96) is a contrasting vision both of the river and
of a bridge. The river is a source of industry, not relaxation. The bridge is a dark
threatening frame across the top half of the painting. In *The Bridge at Argenteuil* the
river is peaceful and the bridge a complement to it.

THE BRIDGE AT
ARGENTEUIL
1874
CELIMAGE.SA/EDIMEDIA

⬅ What makes this landscape dramatic is the railway bridge in the background. Its
presence dominates the painting and forms a solid structure that spans the canvas.

Its very solidness contrasts with the bushes and the woman—both of which are
curved and rounded shapes—the antithesis of the straight lines of the bridge.
Similarly the green of the grass is fresh and natural compared with the gray of the
bridge. Monet is painting the meeting of modernity with tradition. The line of the
bridge is echoed in the line of the horizon. However, the natural and modern worlds
are not harmonized in the same way as they are in *Waterloo Bridge* (1902). In this
painting, bridge, water, and sky merge together. The focal point is the patch of
sunlight on the water rather than the bridge. Even the smoking chimney stack in the
background seems to be a balanced part of the painting.

It is interesting to note that in the 1874 picture, Monet deliberately chose this
view of the bridge so that it did not include the factories that lay just to the left of
where the canvas ends. For *The Bridge at Argenteuil*, he obviously felt that he could
not harmonize industry into a natural background as he had learnt to do when he
painted *Waterloo Bridge*.

Unloading Coal

UNLOADING COAL

1875

MUSEE D'ORSAY, PARIS.
CELIMAGE.SA/EDIMEDIA

← Painted just outside Argenteuil, this picture is unique in Monet's work: it is the only one of his paintings that depicts laborers at work. The result is a dramatic painting that has a schematic composition to it.

A sense of mechanization is achieved by the regular spacing and number of men walking up and down the planks. The men are a part of the machine. The regularity of their movement and the depiction of industrial work going on are countered by the casual passers-by on the bridge. This subject is a very marked contrast to the idyllic boating paintings from the same period. The color scheme is dark and gloomy compared with their lighter tones. However, although illustrating an industrial scene, Monet does achieve a harmony and balance through his use of the vertical and horizontal. The bridge forms a strong network of grid lines that provides a frame over the entire picture.

The men moving across the planks are a strong vertical balance to the horizontal lines of the planks. The overall effect is to create an order within the painting that harmonizes the picture and adds to its machine qualities.

THE JAPANESE WOMAN

1875

BOSTON MUSEUM OF ART,
BOSTON.
CELIMAGE.SA/EDIMEDIA

➡ Included in the second Impressionist exhibition, this work was an abrupt departure from the style that Monet had been cultivating over the preceding decade. At the time it caused a sensation. One critic praised its "solid coloring" and "emphatic impasto."

It harks back to *Camille, or the Woman in the Green Dress* (1866), which was painted in a style that the Salon would appreciate. Monet was very poor at this time, and one theory holds that he deliberately chose to paint a conventionally posed portrait that would have a high chance of selling, with perhaps the added benefit of attracting a new patron. Monet's strong commercial instinct lies behind some of his choices of subject matter and style.

The careful composition and posing of Camille in this painting lack all the spontaneity that Monet had been looking to capture in other works. Camille is not true to life, since she is wearing a blonde wig. The robe itself is magnificent, and Monet's depiction of the samurai warrior contrasts with the sweetness of Camille's face. Monet's interest in Japanese art, which had influenced some of his earlier work, was obviously still strong at this time.

A CORNER OF THE
APARTMENT
1875
MUSEE D'ORSAY, PARIS.
CELIMAGE.SA/LESSING ARCHIVE

◄ In this painting, Monet experiments with a pictorial frame around the subject.
The shapes of the curtains and plants in the foreground are repeated in the curtains
of the background. The frame has the dual purpose of drawing the eye forward and
also adding to the perception of the subject. By making the frame well lit compared
with the subject, Monet emphasizes the darkness of the room.

He is clearly experimenting with light and dark. Jean Monet, who stands at the
center, is one of the darkest patches on the canvas, the light reflecting from the
floor at his feet emphasizing his darkness.

Jean Monet is isolated in the room and is separated from the woman at the
table. He makes a disturbing figure because he is painted so dark and because of the
steady gaze he directs at the viewer. Madame Monet has a similar direct gaze, but
hers is a more intimate, loving look. Jean Monet is also vulnerable; his size is
exaggeratedly small when compared with the height of the plants, which appear to
threaten to engulf him.

A Field of Poppies

A FIELD OF POPPIES

undated

MUSEE DES BEAUX-ARTS, ROUEN.
CELIMAGE.SA/LESSING ARCHIVE

⬅ What the viewer finds so instantly appealing about this painting is the bold colors frequently used by Monet in his landscapes. The contrasting red-green palette gives an interesting and exciting aspect to the painting, once again bringing the landscape to life by capturing the effects of a brilliant summer's day with the bright blue sky and flourishing flora.

A Field of Poppies is a compilation of finer, more confined brushstrokes, which outline the detail of the flowers. By contrast, longer, more generous and relaxed brushstrokes depict the fields and sky in the background. Our eyes can trail from the concentration of color in the foreground, to the more relaxed and smooth area of the backdrop.

As with many of Monet's landscapes, *A Field of Poppies* should be viewed from a distance in order to gain a full appreciation of it. Monet has deliberately altered his brushstroke to provide a generous perspective.

The village houses are intertwined with the trees, becoming part of the natural landscape that consumes them. This was what Monet often did in his paintings, for example *Lunch on the Grass* (1865) (see page 37) and *Lunch* (c. 1873–74) (see page 86), where the figures almost disappear into the trees around them.

WOMEN AMID
FLOWERS

1875

NARODNI GALERIE, PRAGUE.
CELIMAGE.SA/LESSING ARCHIVE

Women amid Flowers is an extravagant declaration of Monet's artistic ability. His wild and vivid use of color on the canvas is stunning. The two female figures in the painting are almost totally consumed by a wash of bright color. We can almost compare this adornment of the canvas to that employed by Gustav Klimt (1862–1918), who used a wild confluence of color to decorate the figures in his paintings and collages.

This picture is a prime example of Monet's impressionistic style. The small, hasty brushstrokes are felt through the paint, bringing the flowers to life. Swift strokes of varying color lie side by side, and the lack of tonal variation makes this even more obvious. Monet hoped that his technique would enable the observer to appreciate the scene in its natural element.

Looking closely at this canvas, it is possible to become lost in a puzzle of color and brushstroke. To be appreciated to its fullest extent, *Women amid Flowers* needs to be considered from a distance.

There is no particular emphasis in this piece. It is as though the status of the women is no greater than that of the plants that surround them. The detail of their dress and their expressions is minimal, furthering the painting's naturalistic effect.

ARGENTEUIL
1875

MUSEE DE L'ORANGERIE, PARIS.
CELIMAGE.SA/LESSING ARCHIVE

➡ Argenteuil was the setting for many of Monet's paintings. This piece displays the same juxtaposition of color found in so much of his work. Here it is found between the red of the boat and the green of the moss. Both of these strong shades are further contrasted by the pale blue color of the water. Lighter shades of the green and blue are reflected in the sky, giving an element of continuity to the painting. This piece is thoughtfully and beautifully compiled in terms of its palette.

Unusually for a waterscape by Monet, the artist has included people, who appear off a small pier to the left of the canvas. The colors used to represent the figures are repeated in their surroundings, serving to incorporate them fully into the painting. This, of course, is a deliberate construct of the artist, who chose to use the same palette and method of brushstroke in order to camouflage the "unnatural" people in a natural environment. They could easily go unnoticed. In addition to these two figures, there is another person to be found on the boat nearby. The features of the figures are blurred and, since they are near the water, Monet has chosen to paint their attire green, to match the tone of the moss floating on the water's surface.

The two red boats in the center act as a main focal point for the painting, although visually the piece seems quite busy, as a result of Monet's use of color. In *Argenteuil*, this seems to be the prevailing aspect of the work.

STREETSIDE OF
ST LAZARE
RAILWAY STATION
(seen toward the
tunnel of Batignolles)
1877

PRIVATE COLLECTION, FRANCE.
CELIMAGE.SA/LESSING ARCHIVE

⬆ A keystone of successful industrial development, the railway features again in this painting, as Monet depicts Paris as a bustling and developed city. Here he creates a very busy, action-filled scene. The image is almost entirely dominated by overwhelming clouds of smoke, through which we can identify a moving train, masses of people, and large buildings in the background, all of which are recognized as defining features of a place at the forefront of industrial development. This notion is furthered by the rapid brushstroke which creates a sense of motion and speed. The artist has achieved an almost granulated effect with the oils, which is particularly noticeable along the tracks and on the station building. As in *Boulevard des Capucines* (1873) (see page 82) Monet reduces the human forms to indistinct shapes, depicting them with a complete lack of detail.

There is a spontaneity here, as a scene is captured that will never be repeated in the same way. Everything is moving, from the train to the swirls of billowing smoke.

Monet produced few industrial scenes in his career, preferring to concentrate on the quieter settings of rural landscapes, or the modern buildings of cities. Thus, *St Lazare Railway Station, The Semaphores* is quite a rare display for the artist, since he painted only a small number of scenes from railway stations.

In this artwork, the palette appears quite dull and gray, although this choice seems an appropriate mix for such a scene. However, the application of color is very different from that found in many of his landscapes. The paint has been applied more solidly, with less frequent and more defined brushstrokes.

A noteworthy aspect of this painting is the sky. Here Monet has achieved an interesting effect, almost as if he were applying the paint over wax to leave dancing white lines across the canvas. The rest of the sky is touched with shades of red and blue, which complement the gray of the objects and buildings. However, these tones are not repeated in the ground, which remains a kind of golden brown.

ST LAZARE
RAILWAY STATION,
THE SEMAPHORES
1877
NIEDERSAECHSISCHES
LANDESMUSEUM, HANOVER.
CELIMAGE.SA/LESSING ARCHIVE

THE STAIRS
1878

➡ This painting is one that was sold to an American buyer, although later it was bought back by the collector Durand-Ruel. America proved to be a profitable market for the Impressionists, thanks to Durand-Ruel, who opened it up to them through exhibitions at which their work was shown.

The appeal of *The Stairs* lies in its subject matter and composition. The stairs leading up are inviting, while the archway provides a provocative glimpse into the courtyard. This is in contrast to *Vétheuil* (1901), where the town is seen from a distance and the viewer is set apart from the town by an expanse of water. *The Stairs* is an intimate and inviting view of a building at close hand, with the viewer now at the heart of the town, not apart from it. *The Stairs* is unusual for its choice of an everyday rural building as its subject. Most Monet paintings of buildings are depicting either modern or Gothic architecture or a group of buildings seen from a distance, as in *Vétheuil*.

The warm pinks and golden colors used combine with the deep blue of the sky to create the effect of a balmy, lazy summer's day. Even the shadow falling across the bottom left-hand corner of the painting does not detract from the warmth.

APPLE TREES NEAR
VETHEUIL
1878
CELIMAGE.SA/LESSING ARCHIVE

← This painting depicts the view down into the valley of Vienne-en-Artheis. It is typical of the rural scenes that Monet produced once he moved to Vétheuil. There is no evidence of industrialization in this painting, which instead focuses on the apple trees in the foreground.

Monet uses small brushstrokes of differing colors on the trees to create the effect of sunlight falling across the blossoms. These smaller strokes gradually become longer as Monet moves down into the valley on the canvas. These longer strokes have the effect of merging colors together and creating a blurring of lines so that the trees in the foreground appear to be strongly in focus compared with the valley in the background.

The critic Philippe Birty saw this painting exhibited at Durand-Ruel's gallery, along with others by Monet. His response was as follows: "It is from afar that these paintings must be judged, and the nearsighted and insensitive will only perceive a confused, mixed-up, tough, or shaggy surface resembling the underside of a Gobelin tapestry with an excessive use of chromium-yellows and orange-yellows." The belief that Monet's paintings are best viewed from a distance still persists among critics today.

PORTRAIT OF MICHEL
MONET AS A BABY
1878–79

CELIMAGE.SA/LESSING ARCHIVE

➡ This painting was produced not long after Michel was born. He still has the full cheeks of a very young baby, although he does have a lot of hair. Despite the quick brushwork, Monet succeeds in creating an impression of Michel that is immediately recognizable as the same child in later portraits.

This style of creating an impression of the person rather than producing a detailed portrait was a change from his earlier work; Monet treats his portraits from this period in the same style as his landscapes. There are a number of portraits of his sons from around this period. His family had until this date often featured as the human presence in many of his landscapes. However, from around 1880 onward Monet included people less and less frequently in his landscapes, which might explain his desire to record them in portraits.

The portrait of Michel is intimate and does not attempt to exaggerate any features or to caricature the child. When looking at Michel's portrait, there is no indication as yet of his character or personality.

THE CHURCH AT VETHEUIL, IN SNOW

1879

MUSEE DU LOUVRE, PARIS.
CELIMAGE.SA/EDIMEDIA

⬆ *The Church at Vétheuil, in Snow* is a somber work that is very different from some of Monet's summer paintings in Vétheuil. The palette of colors used is extremely restricted, offering very little relief from the white and dark colors. *The Garden at Vétheuil* (1881) provides a useful contrast to demonstrate how tightly controlled this palette was.

Matching this rigid color scheme, Monet adheres equally doggedly to the rules of symmetry. The bank forms a solid horizontal line that is repeated in the hedgerow growing above, counterbalanced by the vertical of the church tower and the poplar trees. The buildings all form solid shapes on the canvas, making a pattern of oblongs, squares, and triangles. In *The Garden at Vétheuil*, the house, veranda, and steps form similar shapes on the canvas and attempt to replicate the balance of horizontals and verticals. However, this is disrupted by the garden with the strong twisting shape of the tree dominating the rigid shape of the house.

Some relief from the rigidity of the painting is provided by the short broken brushstrokes used to create the water surface; these help to soften the impact of the flatter bank above.

THE SEINE NEAR VETHEUIL

1879

MUSEE DES BEAUX-ARTS, ROUEN.
CELIMAGE.SA/LESSING ARCHIVES

➡ *The Seine near Vétheuil* is quite dreamy, with an eerie blue-pink overcast, a dark and looming tree tinged with specks of black paint, and a complete absence of human figures. Monet's traditional impressionistic and loose definition of objects creates a scene almost completely unencumbered by the non-natural world. The horizon is also difficult to decipher, and we strain to find a point of recognition.

The Seine is portrayed in a very solemn and somber manner, although a distinct and remarkable compositional and tonal balance is realized in the painting. Monet successfully incorporates all of the different elements of this work into a fine visual representation. Using a familiar technique, he intertwines fragments of color from the trees, the water, and the sky so that they reflect each other, providing a subconscious and intrinsic equilibrium.

As with many of Monet's landscapes and waterscapes, this picture should be viewed from a distance in order to appreciate its full artistic and aesthetic strengths. If the viewer is too close, justice cannot be done to it. The use of longer brushstrokes serves to merge the different colors and create an element of continuity that can be fully appreciated only from a distance.

CAMILLE MONET
(1847–79),
FIRST WIFE OF THE
PAINTER, ON HER
DEATHBED
1879

MUSEE D'ORSAY, PARIS.
CELIMAGE.SA/LESSING ARCHIVE

➡ This picture is powerful and totally encapsulating. The fact that we know it is of the artist's wife, Camille, on her deathbed, makes it all the more compassionate. Monet often painted his wife with a perfect blend of peacefulness and beauty, different from that found in any of his landscapes. In this portrait, Camille is presented with a delicate and thoughtful consideration. To the right of the canvas, a light shines in and settles lightly on the pillow she rests on. This soft, pale pink-yellow gives a further gentleness to the subject.

In another sense, however, Camille is almost unrecognizable in this portrait, since Monet uses subtly different shades of the same color throughout the canvas, even for her face. The long, unfiltered brushstrokes incorporate her figure, making it seem as though she is being consumed or suffocated by the bed she lies upon. Her features, too, are ill-defined. Looking closely, one can just about determine that her eyes are closed, and her mouth is slightly ajar.

Monet's choice of color here is appropriate for the mood of the piece, although it might be regarded as bestowing a kind of angelic quality on the subject.

PORTRAIT OF THE YOUNG BLANCHE HOSCHEDE

1880

MUSEE DES ARTS, ROUEN.
CELIMAGE.SA/LESSING ARCHIVE

➡ Blanche Hoschedé was 14 when this portrait was painted. It is the essence of a young girl, her rosy cheeks, bright eyes, and red lips making her the stereotype of youth. Monet painted a number of portraits of his extended family at this time, although few of his family were featured in his landscape work during this period.

This portrait is very different from that of Camille made 14 years earlier. The style is more in keeping with Monet's Impressionism. The brushwork is more obvious across the portrait, whereas *Camille with a Little Dog* (1866) (see page 46) has this type of brushwork only on the dog. There is a merging of colors across the whole painting, so that there is a blurred effect that is especially noticeable on Blanche's dress. Although her features are clear, they are not painted in the same sharp style as Camille's. Blanche is painted with a strongly patterned wallpaper behind her that prevents her figure from dominating in this painting in the same way that Camille does.

The colors used are mostly pastels, but the red of the hat attracts the eye. This color helps to emphasize Blanche's red lips, but it also distracts the viewer's gaze away from the face. Blanche is painted as part of an overall design, Camille as a separate entity.

PORTRAIT OF MICHEL
IN A POMPOM HAT
1880

MUSEE MARMOTTAN, PARIS.
CELIMAGE.SA/LESSING ARCHIVE

⬅ Michel Monet was Monet's second son with Camille. At the time of this portrait he was two years old. Monet's initial uncertainty about fatherhood had gone by the time Michel was born. Both this portrait and *Portrait of Jean Monet* (1880) (see page 126) are testimony to the love that he felt for his children.

In Michel's portrait, the two-year-old sat apparently docile while his father painted him. The quick brushstrokes, used on the red coat and the red of the boy's cheeks in particular, suggest that Monet at least wanted to create the impression of the portrait having been dashed off. This is especially noticeable when compared to the shorter strokes used on Jean's portrait. Although Michel's features are identifiable, the nose, lips, and eyes are not painted in as much detail as the features in Jean's portrait.

Both paintings share an anonymity of background. A blanket color has been applied so that the focus of the paintings is genuinely the boys. In some of Monet's portraits of fashionable women, the background and clothing are given as much detail as the face and body of the woman. This makes a statement about how the women are perceived. With both of these portraits the individual child is the center of attention.

Portrait of Jean Monet

PORTRAIT OF
JEAN MONET
1880

MUSEE MARMOTTAN, PARIS.
CELIMAGE.SA/LESSING ARCHIVE

◧ Jean Monet would have been around the age of 13 when this portrait was made. Monet had used Jean frequently in landscape paintings before this, sometimes with Camille and sometimes on his own. However, in all of these, he can be identified only as a small child rather than as an individual in his own right.

This portrait is entirely concerned with Jean as Jean. Care is taken to record his features, and he is painted as a full-face portrait. When compared with some of Monet's portraits of society ladies, the intimacy of *Portrait of Jean Monet* is understood. Monet is recording Jean in a very personal style. The lack of detail in the background indicates clearly that Monet is interested in illustrating the individual that is Jean.

Monet's style has changed in the years between these paintings. The brushstrokes are thicker, and he is not afraid to use blocks of color solidly placed on the canvas. No attempt is made to provide a variety of shading on Jean's clothing, as had been done in other portraits.

BOUQUET OF
SUNFLOWERS

1880

METROPOLITAN MUSEUM
OF ART, NEW YORK.
CELIMAGE.SA/LESSING ARCHIVE

➡ In this painting we are immediately drawn into Monet's bold use of color. His
depiction of the sunflowers can be likened to Vincent van Gogh's *Sunflowers*, with
their luscious brushstrokes and bright color. What is a simple still life turns into an
artistically and aesthetically hypnotizing visual masterpiece. *Bouquet of Sunflowers*
is also appealing because of its subject matter and balanced composition. Both
works are very inviting.

There is no distance between the viewer and the vase of flowers, so we are
launched directly into the heart of the image, and are invited to confront the artist's
wonderful array of color. The golden yellow, used in conjunction with a warm
red color, is set against a pale gray-blue background, which creates an unusual
sense of comfort and depth. The flowers are raised toward us, achieving a kind of
three-dimensionality.

As one would expect in a painting by Monet, there is an assertive and lively
quality to *Bouquet of Sunflowers*. The contrasting palette of red and green, coupled
with Monet's artistic technique, make the flowers seem as though they are still in
bloom, since they are richly conveyed in their fullest form.

THE ICE FLOES

1880

MUSEE DES BEAUX-ARTS, LILLE.
CELIMAGE.SA/LESSING ARCHIVE

◄ A complete contrast to the Giverny paintings that were to emerge in the latter
part of this decade, *The Ice Floes* is a very cold and wintry image, delivered through a
flowerless line of trees, a cool palette of blue, purple, and gray tones, and a
collection of piled up and floating ice slabs littering the surface of the river.

There is a line of trees along the water's edge, dominated by a single frail tree
and one that has fallen across the path of the others. This creates a dramatic scene
with a destructive edge.

This is another painting without people and, as in many of Monet's river
paintings, there is no clear definition between the water and the sky, since they both
seem to merge quietly into one another. Another constant feature of these paintings
is the photographic realism of the water, which in this piece appears quite brown
and murky. The colors of the ice slabs creeping in from the bottom left of the canvas
seem quite misplaced in the context of the painting, owing to their unusual green
tone and unrealistic block-like appearance. The buildings lining the river and the
boat on the water are devoid of color and reduced to the black silhouettes of their
forms. However, at a closer glance, one can detect hints of green in the houses,
reflecting the color that appears so overtly in the ice slabs, creating an unexpected
balance between the two.

ICE FLOES ON THE SEINE
1880

MUSEE D'ORSAY, PARIS.
CELIMAGE.SA/LESSING ARCHIVE

➡ Probably the main feature of this work is the water. Looking at the painting, we are on a level with the river, and it fills our vision as it flows toward us and runs along the bottom edge of the canvas. It is as though we are on a boat overlooking the ice as it floats aimlessly across the water. Looking up toward the sky, we can draw similarities between the tone and brushwork of the two areas.

At the end of our view of the water is a line of trees, all varying in height, but standing strangely straight and still. They have a certain glow about them, as they are brushed with a warm red-green. This color is reflected in the water, and asserts the division between the river and the sky, which otherwise would become merged in one canvas of color. Their long, wavy reflections also provide the only source of movement on the water's surface. Otherwise, the ice just seems to stand still in its tracks, without causing any rippling effect.

The overall effect of this painting is another quite cold presentation of the Seine, produced with a familiar cool palette and method of brushstroke. However, somewhere in the stillness of *Ice Floes on the Seine* lies a soft unspoken beauty, hidden in the warmth of the trees.

133

Still Life with Fruit

STILL LIFE WITH FRUIT

1880

KUNSTHALLE, HAMBURG.

CELIMAGE.SA/LESSING ARCHIVE

◄ This is a rare opportunity to glimpse one of the few still lifes that Monet produced. This piece is rich aesthetically, since the artist realistically and skillfully depicts the different fruits in their natural, rich colors, while retaining an emphasis on their form and composition within the arrangement as a whole. Thus, we can see how Monet treated his still lifes in a similar way to his landscapes. In *Still Life With Fruit* he deliberately places objects of complementary and contrasting colors together, in order to convey the rich blend that we see in many of his waterscapes from Giverny. The objects are carefully arranged to provide a balance to the artwork.

The wealth and intensity of the tone and light used to address the grapes in this piece give them a striking realism. They trail across the rest of the fruit, leading our eyes across to the pears and apples, which they adorn. Compositionally, they also provide a spine to the still life, as a dramatic focal point.

A secondary focus is created by the two bright red apples, set aside from the main assortment close to the front of the table. Set against the green plants, these two pieces of fruit attract our attention.

The tablecloth and background color are less obvious because of their neutrality and regular brushstroke, although they both serve to highlight the arrangement and increase its striking effect on the observer.

⬆ This painting epitomizes the Impressionist period. It is as though the sun is mourning a lifeless scene. The blackness of the tree and the mound on which it stands, with a kind of cross-hatched, matchstick effect on the horizon, combine to create a barren, possibly war-stricken scene.

The painting achieves perspective through the distant naked sun, which also provides a focal point for the work as a whole. The reflective line it creates across the water also draws our attention to the bright red circle hovering just above the landscape. The sky and water are touched by its rays, and Monet again reflects the color of the sky in the water to provide a sense of continuity to the entire work.

In the early 1870s, Claude Monet moved to Paris to escape the Franco-Prussian War. Here, he studied the English masters John Constable (1776–1837) and Joseph Mallord William Turner (1775–1851), two artists whose influence we can see in this particular painting. The effect achieved by the red haze in the sky can be likened to that created by Turner, who filled his canvases with warm and intense colors.

The only contrast in the painting is given by the green haze, which hangs loosely above the water, distorting our view of the horizon but also providing a sense of depth.

SETTING SUN ON THE SEINE AT LAVACOURT, EFFECT OF WINTER

1880

MUSEE DU PETIT PALAIS, PARIS. CELIMAGE.SA/LESSING ARCHIVE

⬅ In order to paint this picture, Monet made a great effort to reach the exact location that he thought was necessary for the best viewpoint. It is recorded that he was seen clambering over cliffs and rocks dragging six or seven canvases with him. This would be in keeping with his ideals concerning the *plein-air* technique, although the reality was that he finished most of the canvases in his studio.

Fishing Boats in front of the Beach and the Cliffs of Pourville and *The Cliffs at St Adresse* (1873) (see page 81) seem to lack some of the obvious spontaneity evident in other paintings, although the scurrying clouds in the former have some sense of being captured on canvas on location. The painting depicts sailing boats, which had already proved a popular subject when Monet lived at Argenteuil. Here the lonely figure on the shore is isolated by being detached from the fun of the boats at sea. This isolation is emphasized by the careful blocking Monet adopts with each element. Strong lines separate the shore from the sea and the sea from the sky. There is no blurring of the boundaries in either painting, as has been seen in other works. Instead, each element is clearly differentiated from its neighbor.

FISHING BOATS IN FRONT OF THE BEACH AND THE CLIFFS OF POURVILLE

1882

CELIMAGE.SA/LESSING ARCHIVE

PATH THROUGH THE
CORN AT POURVILLE
1882

◄ What is most noticeable about this painting is the strong, bright coloring. The blue of the sea is reminiscent of some of Monet's paintings from the Mediterranean. What he set out to do was to capture the effects of a brilliant summer's day on the beach landscape.

By using strong colors that contrast with each other rather than blend together, he achieves the effect of each color appearing even stronger. Thus, where the red of the wheat touches the blue of the sea, each benefits from the contrast; the same is true where the sea meets the shore. This time the effect of the sun is to render the sand a brilliant white. These blocks of color work together to create an impression on the viewer. There is actually very little detail in the picture itself.

This painting has strong lines that form horizontals and verticals. In the picture the curved path not only draws the eye toward the sea but also provides a vertical curve that meets the sand and continues to the horizon. This balances the horizontal created by the sea and the cliff.

Claude Monet

Monet painted several scenes like this during his early years as an artist. He usually adopted a bird's-eye perspective when depicting buildings in his works, which allowed a certain emphasis on the medium and the brushstroke, as well as on the content of the painting itself. *The Shack of the Customs Officials* is very expressive in terms of its method. The sea in the foreground and distance, and the shrubbery leading up to the shack have been executed with an extravagant application of the paintbrush and medium. This gives the painting a sprawling motion, which, at first glance, confuses our vision, as the colors of the water blend and almost reach into the sky, distorting our horizon.

Amid the areas of green, Monet uses splashes of black and gray to create shadow and tonal variation. The shack itself is painted in a similar way, except that it has white highlights to accentuate its angles and height. Here, we can see Monet's close attention to color and its effects. It is a picturesque scene, executed in a mild palette, creating the feeling of serenity so often found in Monet's works.

THE SHACK OF THE CUSTOMS OFFICIALS, EFFECT OF THE AFTERNOON
1882
MUSEE DES DOUANES, BORDEAUX.
CELIMAGE.SA/LESSING ARCHIVE

This piece explores a wide palette of color and tone. Colors appear in a rainbow-like fashion, with a picturesque view out across the water. A rich and intense use of color draws us into this intimate scene. The piece demonstrates the versatility of the artist. Monet, with his powerful, ever alert eye, was able to paint not only the most vibrant and brilliant pictures, but also rather gray and gloomy landscapes, formulated in neutral tones. Here certain elements of the bushes are highlighted by specks of yellow paint. In the case of the deep green bush in the near distance in particular, this helps to provide a realistic color and depth. It also serves to break up larger areas of lighter green. We can admire Monet's use of color and his experimentation with technique in this painting.

Unlike in his boat scenes, where the canvas is dominated by the subject rather than the sky, in *Path to La Cavée, Pourville*, only a fine run of sky frames the rim of the canvas, before we are launched into the bushes to witness this spectacular view out to sea.

PATH TO LA CAVEE, POURVILLE
1882
MUSEUM OF FINE ARTS, BOSTON.
CELIMAGE.SA/LESSING ARCHIVE

ETRETAT: THE BEACH
AND PORT D'AMONT
1883

MUSEE D'ORSAY, PARIS.
CELIMAGE.SA/LESSING ARCHIVE

➡ Monet adopts an aerial perspective to paint this piece, as he usually did when painting such scenes, to create a grander or more dramatic effect. Here the additional height that the painter gains over the beach makes the figures appear small and insignificant in relation to the cliff that reaches above them. The painted edge of the cliff is smoother, giving the whole picture a softer feel.

Again, this is an impressionistic work and so there tends to be a lack of detail in the figures and the boats. The people are so small, in fact, that they could easily be overlooked in favor of the dominating rock face in the background. This fills half of our view of the sky and ends somewhere off the edge of the canvas. However, it also serves to provide a balance to the boats in the foreground. Almost identical tones and technique are used to complete the sea and the sky.

In this painting Monet depicts a familiar holiday or family scene, which is aesthetically pleasing to the eye. Because of this, it is likely that *Etretat: The Beach and Port d'Amont* would have sold readily at the time it was produced. The bold colors that have been used for the vessels separates this painting from many of Monet's previous seascapes.

The boats seem more defined than the background cliff and water, which works to reduce the spontaneity of the piece slightly, but not so much that we lose its overall impression. The lucidity and flow of the brushstrokes in the sky and sea create a sense of being captured on canvas on location.

◄ *Storm at Etretat* was painted in the same year that Monet moved to Giverny, along the River Seine. Apart from a couple of trips abroad in his later years, he would spend the rest of his life here. This is one of several paintings that provide evidence of Monet's long obsession with coastal storms.

The artwork is sprawling with motion, as Monet successfully generates a cool palette with a fiery quality. The waves hurl themselves at the shore, fringed with a brilliant white, cream, and pink color, enhancing the effect of the storm. The two small, silhouetted figures stand close to the stormy waves in front of them, reinforcing the weather's threatening character.

This is a very dark image, full of deep blue and gray color, used to convey the image of a storm on its progress. The palette in this piece works in complete contrast to that in works such as *Path to La Cavée, Pourville* (1882) (see page 144). This shows how Monet exercised such a truly commendable, varied, and skillful monopoly of color throughout his career.

VILLAS AT BORDIGHERA, ITALY
undated

⬆ This piece is compositionally and aesthetically buzzing. The wild slanted brushstrokes form plenty of images across the canvas. Our focus is drawn to the villa on the right-hand side of the picture, but also to the bright slim trunk of the tree in the center. The curve of the tree is counterbalanced by the very straight edge of the villa, emphasized by a gray shadow creeping round the side of the building. There appears to be quite a strong contrast between the wild growth of the flora and the stark whiteness of the villas at the left-hand side of our view. The absence of people in this landscape is quite obvious, almost imposing. The artist denies the importance of man, and instead suggests that nature is reclaiming the land.

In terms of color, *Villas at Bordighera* boasts a wide palette of blues, reds, greens, browns, and different shades of white and gray. Unlike in several of Monet's Seine paintings, bright shades creep toward the forefront of the canvas, creating a beautiful scene of vigorous color and shade.

⬆ This picture is full of energy and color. The roughness of the rocks complements the uneven brushstrokes used on the sea. The strokes are laid on quickly and thickly, the sea has occasional broad white dashes of color on it to represent the waves and the horizontal lines of the sea contrast with the rocks, with brushstrokes painted in several directions. The trees provide the vertical line that balances the horizon. The horizontal and vertical are particularly emphasized in this painting by the contrasting techniques used on the sky, sea, and trees. The sky is painted as a smooth surface, making use of pale colors; the sea and trees are painted in stronger colors using shorter brushstrokes, and a definite line is formed where they each meet the sky.

On the sea a single vertical white line is highlighted against the pink skyline, representing a sail. When compared with his earlier paintings of boats it is obvious how Monet's technique and composition have changed. By 1884, he was content to represent the boat as a dash of white paint, an impression on the horizon.

CAP MARTIN
1884

MUSEE DES BEAUX ARTS,
TOURNAI.
CELIMAGE.SA/LESSING ARCHIVE

Claude Monet

ETRETAT, CLIFF:
FISHING BOATS
LEAVING THE HARBOR

1885

MUSEE DES BEAUX-ARTS, DIJON.
CELIMAGE.SA/LESSING ARCHIVE

◧ This is is one of several paintings of Etretat that Monet produced. Usually, they would feature the dramatic cliffs and needles—however, this piece seems gloomy and somewhat cold and icy in the colors of its execution. Monet forms the cliffs with a loose outline, making it appear unthreatening to the small fishing boats in the water. Instead, it looms as a soft gray mass in the distance.

The arch is almost a sketchy cutout and the boats seem precariously dotted around the surface of the water. In terms of color, there is an uncomfortable balance between the gloomy gray of the cliffs and the more delicate and hypnotic turquoise of the sea. There is a further contrast between the calmness of the water, with its lukewarm green color, and the red sails of the boats. These act as a point of focus in the painting, as we follow their path toward the cliffs.

Yet, there is also a notable harmony to this composition. Monet's application of color is lucid, as he makes a remote use of detail to outline the painting's features, thus capturing an air of stillness within the painting.

GLADIOLI
1882–85
PRIVATE COLLECTION, PARIS.
CELIMAGE.SA/EDIMEDIA

◄ The agent Durand-Ruel commissioned Monet to paint a set of decorative panels;
it took the artist over two years to complete them. They each depicted either fruit or
flowers and were designed to reflect the changing seasons.

The shape of the gladioli is perfect for an upright panel. Painted positioned on
what appears to be a table, the background is very simple, unlike in
Chrysanthemums (1878), where the wallpaper pattern is clearly in evidence behind
the flowers. By placing the gladioli against a blue background the colors of the
flowers are revealed to startling effect. In contrast, the chrysanthemums lose out to
the effect created by the flowers on the wallpaper. Whereas the chrysanthemums
move across the canvas, the gladioli form vertical lines counterbalanced by the edge
of the table.

The strange vase in which the flowers are presented forms a second focal point,
drawing the eye away from the gladioli and down the canvas to the white flowers
on the vase. The vertical linear rhythm of the gladioli painting is pleasing to the eye.

THE CHURCH AT
BELLECOEUR
1885

CELIMAGE.SA/LESSING ARCHIVE

➡ Painted only a few years apart, both *The Church at Bellecoeur* and *The Stairs* (1878) (see page 110) are intimate, close views of a rural setting. Both are devoid of people and concentrate on the beauty of the buildings. In *The Church at Bellecoeur* Monet shows a little more of the village, which seems sleepy in the warm sun.

The difference between the two paintings is that *The Church at Bellecoeur* appears to have a greater preoccupation with shapes and patterns than does *The Stairs*. The buildings form a pattern of oblongs, squares, and triangles. They are all, apart from the church, depicted with the slant of their roofs facing the viewer, creating a contrast between the red of the roof and the white of the walls that emphasizes the geometric shapes. The low walls running around the properties echo this. *The Stairs* does have a similar pattern with its walls and roof, but because the viewer is positioned closer to a single building this pattern is more difficult to discern.

In *The Church at Bellecoeur* the clouds in the sky provide a contrast to the regular shapes below. The tree in the foreground also helps to disrupt the regularity of the pattern. The amount of space given over to the blue sky helps to prevent the complex of buildings overwhelming the painting.

STORM ON THE COAST
OF BELLE-ILE
1886

MUSEE D'ORSAY, PARIS.
CELIMAGE.SA/SCALA ARCHIVES

➡ Monet found the changing weather conditions on the Brittany coast very exciting. In particular, when the weather was rough, he was impatient to capture the moment on canvas. The swiftness of the brushstrokes in these Belle-Ile paintings adds to the air of dashing the pictures off in a frenzy of excitement.

In both paintings, a sense of drama is created by moving the horizon very high up the canvas, making the sea appear to be flooding into the sky. *Storm on the Coast of Belle-Ile* in particular exaggerates this effect by using similar colors for both the sky and the sea. The swift brushwork on the sea versus the more solid strokes of the sky help the viewer to identify the horizon. In *The Belle-Ile Rocks* (1886) (see page 160) Monet uses a bank of cloud to identify the dividing line.

In *Storm on the Coast of Belle-Ile*, the sea itself is painted with a lot of white. The turbulence of the waves hitting the rocks is the cause of this coloring. Because the painting has been cropped on the left, the viewer feels that he has been placed on a level with this turbulence. In *The Belle-Ile Rocks* the artist's viewpoint is higher, which helps to maintain a distance from the water, leaving the observer removed from the intensity of the action.

THE BELLE-ILE ROCKS
1886

MUSEE D'ORSAY, PARIS.
COURTESY OF EDIMEDIA

➡ The wildness of the sea is captured here by Monet's use of color, the dark blues and greens typical of a stormy day. In contrast, when the sea is viewed on a calm day, as in *The Beach at Pourville, Sunset* (1882), the sea has softer tones. The color of the sea in *The Belle-Ile Rocks* does not indicate a specific time of day, but the end of day is explicit in the 1882 painting.

The drama of this painting lies entirely in the stormy waves of the sea. Their power is complemented by the solid dark mass of the rocks. The movement of the waves is presented by using short brushstrokes and by laying different colors next to each other, so that a dark blue stroke may be placed alongside a green one. In *The Beach at Pourville, Sunset* Monet lengthens the brushstrokes along the surface of the sea to produce a more regular surface and creates the impression of tranquility.

The menacing presence of the rocks actually takes up nearly the same amount of canvas space as the sea. By painting them as encroaching across to the bottom left of the painting, but losing ground to the sea in the top right-hand corner, Monet depicts the eternal battle between land and sea.

⬆ For some critics, this painting is concerned with the nature of girls passing into womanhood. Their looks and bodies are undergoing constant change. This perpetual development is illustrated in the three girls by the lack of features shown. These girls' faces are almost devoid of detail.

Their association with nature is strong. Not only is Monet recording them at the most transient and developmental period in their lives, but, unlike in *Portrait of the Young Blanche Hoschedé* (1880) (see page 122), their clothing identifies them with their natural background. The pink on their dresses is a reflection of the pink in the grassy bank behind the boat. For some critics this is symbolic of nature often being referred to as a female; Monet was using the women as a representation of nature.

Whether this was his aim is impossible to assert. What is certain is that this picture is one of harmony and balance. The boat is balanced by its reflection in the water, and all the colors work together with the subject matter to create a tranquil painting.

IN THE ROWING BOAT
1887
MUSEE D'ORSAY, PARIS.
CELIMAGE.SA/LESSING ARCHIVE

◀ Claude Monet spent his youth in Le Havre, where he first excelled as a caricaturist, before being converted to landscape painting by his early mentor, Boudin.

As with many of Monet's landscapes and waterscapes, this piece shows a wonderful use and application of color. The artist successfully creates motion with color and the canvas is filled with a sea of red and golden yellow. The red tulips provide a blanket of color in the foreground, a technique similar to that found in *Field of Yellow Irises at Giverny* (see page 168), painted a year later in 1887.

As in Monet's *Tulip Field, Holland*, from the same year, 1886, this landscape is dominated not by a series of contours, but rather by an equal split between the sky and the ground. Monet's passion and excitement when painting his landscapes in Holland can be witnessed in his short, broken brushstrokes, consistent with his impressionistic style. In doing this, he hoped to capture an image at an instant in time, recreating its beauty and color. He certainly achieves it in this painting. Emotion emanates from this canvas, almost as an overwhelming force.

A FIELD OF TULIPS
IN HOLLAND
1886
MUSEE D'ORSAY, PARIS.
CELIMAGE.SA/LESSING ARCHIVE

The Garden
at Giverny

**THE GARDEN AT
GIVERNY**

undated

MUSEE D'ORSAY, PARIS.
CELIMAGE.SA/LESSING ARCHIVE

⬅ *The Garden at Giverny* is dominated by a sea of purple color. Our view starts at the bottom of a small, narrow path, which forms a dividing line between two thick blankets of purple flowers. The downward brushstrokes of the trees mimic rainfall, providing an interesting contrast between the more clearly defined flowers that stretch across the floor. Two shades prevail in this painting: green and purple.

A house peers at us from behind the dense layer of trees, although the two flowerbeds remain the focus of our view. There is no sky to dampen the strength of their presence, as in *Field of Yellow Irises at Giverny* (1887) (see page 168). In *The Garden at Giverny*, Monet is conveying the essence of the plants. Another difference between the two works is that *The Garden at Giverny* does not have an obvious linear design, since it lacks the horizontal banding found in so many of Monet's other paintings.

The tone is fairly dark, with the green trees overshadowing the plants and the house. The only relief comes from the little specks of yellow that are dotted around the trees and flowers, representing a source of light in the distance.

⬆ Despite the fact that this painting is entitled *Field of Yellow Irises at Giverny*, two colors dominate, yellow and purple. The purple in the foreground is repeated in the hedges that span the middle of the painting. This is a very different treatment of the iris from that of the later *Yellow Irises* (1924–25). In that painting, the yellow of the flower is the main focus; here its effect has been dampened by being mixed with purple.

A second obvious difference is that the flowers themselves are the primary focus of *Yellow Irises*. Deprived of a background, it is the essence of the plants that Monet is demonstrating. In *Field of Yellow Irises at Giverny*, Monet puts the flowers in their natural habitat with a hedge and sky as background. They have none of the Oriental style that can be found in *Yellow Irises*.

This painting has the horizontal banding found in many other Monet paintings. The field of flowers forms the first band, the hedge the second, and the sky the third. Painted in landscape format, this linear design is very obvious.

FIELD OF YELLOW IRISES AT GIVERNY
1887
MUSEE MARMOTTAN, PARIS.
CELIMAGE.SA/SCALA ARCHIVES

⬅ The figure in the foreground is believed to be Alice Hoschedé, later to become Alice Monet. The two boys following behind are her sons. This is one of the few paintings where Alice acted as model.

A natural scene, it captures the moment when the family is walking from Giverny. This summer outing is a theme that recurs frequently in Monet's work. The warmth of the day is made explicit by the parasol Alice carries; the use of yellow on the field adds to the warmth of the painting. The brushwork reflects the angle of the different planes on which it is used: thus, horizontal brushstrokes are used on the field because it is a flat plane and diagonal ones are used on the hill in the background to emphasize the angle of the slope. Monet is trying to capture the nature of each element not only in terms of its color but also in terms of its substance. The grass seems long and wild in the foreground precisely because it is painted with quick strokes that dart in all directions. This is of more importance to Monet than painting a detailed and accurate picture of the grass.

LIMETZ MEADOW
1887
CELIMAGE.SA/LESSING ARCHIVE

VIEW OF ANTIBES
1888
CELIMAGE.SA/EDIMEDIA

⮕ The trees in the painting frame this distant view of the coastal town of Antibes. The blue of the sea and sky are so similar that they provide a backdrop against which to display the tree. It is the shape of the branches of the tree and its leaves that interests Monet.

The tree in this painting is the highlight, its strong solid trunk and branches contrasting with the soft, almost translucent quality of the leaves. By placing the tree so prominently in the foreground, Monet emphasizes the subtlety of the colors and light that surround the city. The solid structure of the tree makes Antibes dreamlike in contrast. It floats on the water in a wash of flesh, gold, and pink color that creates a haze around it. In contrast, in *Antibes, View of the Cape in the Mistral* (1888) thicker strokes and vibrant colors are used so that Antibes is not surrounded by the same mystical air.

In *View of Antibes* a great deal of space on the canvas is given to the sky, which allows the tree to be highlighted and results in Antibes appearing small and delicate. This is one of four paintings of this composition, which form a mini-series.

ANTIBES, VIEW OF
THE FORT
1888

M.O.M.A., NEW YORK.
CELIMAGE.SA/LESSING ARCHIVE

◄ Monet's motifs are said to shift between the rough and the soft. *Antibes, View of the Fort* is definitely one of his soft subjects. The colors glow with hints of gold, pink, and turquoise.

The harmonization of colors present in this painting would appear again 20 years later in *The Grand Canal and Santa Maria della Salute* (1908). The composition is also very similar. Both paintings feature a large expanse of water in the foreground, a building that appears to be floating on the water's surface, and an expanse of sky above. This similarity arises from Monet's preoccupation with buildings next to water. His treatment of reflection demonstrates how he was fascinated by the effect of light on a solid structure when it is placed by water. The reflection is reduced to color rather than shape, so that the fort's reflection is lines of gold.

The colors used are soft and pastel in tone, with a palette of rose, gold, white, blue, and green. Each part of the picture is painted distinct from its neighbor rather than being merged together.

LANDSCAPE WITH
FIGURES, GIVERNY
1888

COURTESY OF EDIMEDIA

◄ In the second half of the 1880s, Monet returned to figure painting. He painted
16 pictures of his family between 1885 and 1889, striving to capture figures in
a natural background in true *plein-air* style. Monet started trying to achieve
this initially in 1865, with *Lunch on the Grass* (see page 37). His aim was to approach
figure painting in the same spontaneous manner in which he worked
on landscapes.

In the early work he tries to do this by painting the figures as if unrelated to
each other and with strong blocking of color on the women that is unconcerned
with shading. They are caught in the middle of an action rather than in a posed
setting. In *Landscape with Figures, Giverny* there is the same detachment between
the figures. The first and second group are separated by a large space, the three
figures in the foreground apparently unconcerned with each other. The viewer is
positioned uncomfortably close to the three people in the foreground. This unusual
angle adds to the air of spontaneity.

The colors used to signify the figures are repeated in the tones of the grass,
trees, and hills in the background. Here Monet is using color to incorporate the
figures as an integral part of the landscape.

THE CREUSE AT
SUNSET
1889
COURTESY OF EDIMEDIA

⬆ When Monet visited the Massif Central region of France he decided to capture the barren and dramatic landscape around the River Creuse. When he started it was winter. To his horror, while he was still working on the details of a tree, spring arrived, causing the tree to bud. Unable to cope with his subject changing into a green and leafy tree, Monet paid the owner to strip the buds off. Perhaps Monet was not so reactive to nature as he would have liked his public to believe.

The river and the rocks around it appear in many of the pictures of the region. This one depicts the river in the glory of a late afternoon. The effect of the light makes the hills form a dark mass against which the sky and water stand out. The same view in the evening is cooler but allows the features of the hillside to emerge. The bleakness of the area is enhanced by the lack of vegetation, and the only source of warmth comes from the sky. This glow has gone from the hills by the evening.

The barren landscape of the Creuse Valley intrigued Monet, and he sought to capture its savagery. Here the Creuse is empty and cold. The strange blue light of the evening adds to the coldness of the painting. The blue touches the hills and the water. In contrast the hills seem red. They swell up on the canvas to form imposing rounds that seem to be never-ending. The sense of infinity that surrounds them is achieved by having them stretch right across the canvas and by giving them the appearance of forcing the sky back so that only a slim strip is left.

What is interesting about the Creuse paintings is the range of effects Monet creates from the same subject. His study of different light at different times of day produced a set of pictures that come alive through the variety of colors used. Here blue has a strong presence; in others, orange, red, or purple are the dominant colors. In this way Monet maintains the interest of the viewer.

VALLEY OF
THE CREUSE,
EVENING EFFECT
1889

MUSEE MARMOTTAN, PARIS.
CELIMAGE.SA/LESSING ARCHIVE

RIVER BEND
undated

◪ Claude Monet was always at the forefront of artistic development. In looking at the brushstroke, the contrast of colors and the consistency with which he exploited his medium (which he went on to develop and elaborate throughout the long course of his artistic career), we map out how Monet achieved central status in the Impressionist movement. In *River Bend* we witness yet another combination of these elements, which illustrates an artistic method and technique handled with confidence, together with an extravagant use of color.

One of the first things we notice in this painting is the golden, burning red and orange sky, crowning the swirling contours in the distance and almost obscuring our vision of the landscape. Just above the rim of the hills, a bright, shimmering yellow outlines the meeting of earth and sky. The hills themselves are woven through with shades of green, red, brown, and pink, in a style that can be likened to that found in the landscapes of Vincent van Gogh (1853–90).

There is an air of mystery to this piece, as we are confronted with a body of water that stretches behind the hills to an unknown source. Fragments of color from the water are introduced into the hills and a reflection of the sky on the water's surface gives a subconscious unity to the painting.

Poplars

POPLARS ON THE
BANK OF THE EPTE

1891

TATE GALLERY, LONDON.
CELIMAGE.SA/LESSING ARCHIVE

◄ As with the haystack series of paintings, Monet often used poplars in his work. Like the subject of his first series, poplars were of great commercial importance to the rural community. The very trees that Monet was painting were due to be harvested for timber before he had completed the series. Monet struck a deal with the timber merchant, and together they bought them on condition that the merchant left them standing until Monet had completed his series of paintings.

Most of the 24 paintings in the series were made on board Monet's boat studio. They are painted at a point where the river bends back on itself to form an "S," hence the double line of trees. By painting from on board his boat, Monet's vantage point is low, allowing the trees' height to be emphasized. They soar across the painting. The strong vertical trunks are contrasted by the soft curves of the leaves at the top, the billowing clouds echoing the shape of the tops of the trees.

By painting a foreground of water, Monet creates the sensation for viewers that they are floating in the middle of the river. This has been described as a duck's-eye perspective. He is attempting to immerse his viewers into the landscape, as opposed to holding them back from it.

◄ This work is minimalist in terms of its content, yet has the intrinsic beauty of a cool, limited palette and delicate execution.

From the haze of glowing color in the far distance, to the blues of the trees in the foreground, it seems as though we are amid the shade of the foliage and its reflection. This contrasts with what is happening across the horizon, where a thick layer of shrubbery is set alight by a fire of soft red and yellow.

Compositionally the piece is simple yet effective. The trees immediately in front of us are evenly distributed across the length of the canvas, creating a very balanced feel. The trees themselves are equal in terms of their width, and all stretch upward, off the top of the canvas. They form almost perfect and untainted mirror images in the water, as though the reflections are just as real as the trees. The water is thus still, and unaffected by its inhabitants.

The color scheme is limited to a soft palette of blues, browns, greens, yellows, and reds. The warm reds and yellows, set against the pale blue, allow the painting to form an element of depth and contrast, whereas the blue of the water is repeated across the sky, giving the painting a definite sense of continuity and balance.

POPLARS, OR THE
FOUR TREES
1891
METROPOLITAN MUSEUM
OF ART, NEW YORK.
CELIMAGE.SA/LESSING ARCHIVE

◄ This is one of many paintings inspired by Giverny. This scene from the end of summer has a very light and airy feel to it. The haystacks are an appropriate and comfortable image associated with the warm season, and the blurring effect that Monet has chosen to use, together with his blend of colors, makes it seem as though we are being blinded by the sheer power of the sun over the hay. There is an absence of tonal variation, since even the closest edges of the forms cannot be outlined, because of the mirage effect caused by the heat of the sun.

In the distance, this method is continued, as the far-off mass of trees forms a green haze of color. The brushstrokes used to create this piece are small and somewhat erratic, leaving a strong impression on our mind. This, of course, is the intention of the artist as he captures a scene from a lazy summer's day, one particular moment in time, so as to immortalize it.

HAYSTACKS, END OF
SUMMER, GIVERNY
1891
MUSEE D'ORSAY, PARIS.
CELIMAGE.SA/LESSING ARCHIVE

VIEW OF ROUEN NEAR
THE COAST
OF ST CATHERINE
c. 1892
CELIMAGE.SA/LESSING ARCHIVE

◄ This work was probably left unfinished. It is not signed and it is possible to
identify the outlines of buildings that Monet was obviously intending to add in.
However, this does not detract from the work, which is fascinating because of its
choice of subject.

Monet painted very few industrial scenes in his career, preferring quieter rural
landscapes or the modern buildings of cities as subject matter. In this painting and
Unloading Coal (1875) (see page 96), the subject is modern and industrial. The
paintings share a similar palette, so that they have been painted with primarily dark
or subdued colors. This gives the whole scene a somber air. *View of Rouen near the
Coast of St Catherine* lacks the regularity and machine quality that the men evenly
spaced on the ramps provide in *Unloading Coal*. Each man mimics the next in
posture, adding to the balance of the painting.

In *View of Rouen near the Coast of St Catherine* Rouen is shown from a slight
distance and its smoking chimneys feature prominently. This again is unusual.
Chimneys have appeared in other Monet works, but usually they are found in the
background, romanticized by shrouds of fog and smoke. Here they dominate the
skyline, forcing the viewer to acknowledge their presence and providing the pivot
around which the industrial town is set.

Rouen Cathedral

ROUEN CATHEDRAL,
SUNLIGHT EFFECT

1893

CLARK ART INSTITUTE,
WILLIAMSTOWN.
CELIMAGE.SA/LESSING ARCHIVE

◀ Rouen Cathedral became the subject of another series of paintings by Monet, and the first to concentrate so exclusively on an architectural subject. The rationale behind his choice of Rouen Cathedral was in line with his subjects for previous series of paintings, in that it is distinctly French.

Monet's letters of the time describe the struggle he had with his subject: this series took three years to reach exhibition. Monet has abandoned the conventions of setting and taken the viewer uncomfortably close to the cathedral. Monet does not paint in the entire building; only a part of the cathedral is shown. The painting does not dwell on architectural detail but aims to capture the moment. The primary interest is the effect of light on the surface of the building. The cathedral is shown here in full sunlight, which creates a golden glow on the building.

Monet took a year's break between painting this series of pictures and he often painted over sections of a picture again, so the canvases have a crustation of paint. Some critics have found this reminiscent of the actual stonework of the building.

MORNING, WHITE HARMONY

1894

MUSEE D'ORSAY, PARIS.
CELIMAGE.SA/LESSING ARCHIVE

➡ Throughout his artistic career, and particularly in his paintings of Rouen Cathedral, Monet experimented extensively with the effects of light. In doing so, he would often record the same scene or building at different times of the day, in order to see the effect that the light was having on the subject. These works are regarded as among his most memorable, dedicated, and technically crafted works.

In this painting Monet explores the effect of the early morning light on the cathedral, creating a dark, somber, and lucid effect, quite different from that in *Rouen Cathedral, Sunlight Effect* (1893) (see page 190). In this, the cathedral is projected in a light, almost celebratory manner. His application of oils works to complement this approach, the thick and slight brushstrokes accentuating or blurring certain features of the building.

This series of artworks is artistically and architecturally innovative. Monet focuses on a particular area of the cathedral in order to experiment with his artistic techniques, while producing a unique style of art. This was the first occasion on which he focused on the architecture of a building, portraying it in a highly distinctive and progressive way. Monet was often ahead of his contemporaries in terms of his novel and forward-looking artistic experimentation.

ROUEN CATHEDRAL:
HARMONY IN BROWN
undated

MUSEE D'ORSAY, PARIS.
CELIMAGE.SA/LESSING ARCHIVE

➡ This piece is an exploration of Gothic architecture. The shade and detail used by Monet are both complementary and balanced. We approach the cathedral from its base, looking upward at its grand height. We are not invited to view the entire cathedral, however, instead, we focus on this part of it. However, the use of color and tone creates a strong presence, and we face this part of the building from quite an uncomfortable perspective.

Although Monet's studies of Rouen Cathedral concentrate primarily on this one architectural site, the paintings themselves do not focus so heavily on the detail of the building, as much as on the effect that the surrounding light has on it. In *Rouen Cathedral: Harmony in Brown*, Monet records the influence of dark shadows within the overall light upon the church, since the lack of natural light serves to shadow and accentuate certain features of the building. A similar technique is followed in the artist's other cathedral paintings, such as *Rouen Cathedral, Sunlight Effect* (1983) (see page 190), in which Monet engages with the effects of daylight, which, at its full height, works to create a golden haze around the cathedral's features, partially diffusing the detail of its characteristics.

THE SEINE NEAR
GIVERNY
1894

◀ The main feature of this work is the water. The viewer is on a level with the river, which flows forward, drawing the eye along its course. It fills the bottom of the canvas; in fact the water dissects the canvas virtually in a straight line. Above that line its color is reflected in the color of the sky. A comparison of the bottom and top left-hand corners reveals almost identical brushwork and tone.

The land that divides the water and sky prevents them from becoming one. It is only where the land is reflected in the water that any indication of movement on the water's surface occurs. The brushstrokes become long, horizontal lines of varying colors to indicate the ripples, in contrast to the water away from the dark reflection, where the color is almost one block of paint.

There is no sense of perspective. The banding of water, land, and sky is simplified into three broad bands of color. This is broken only by the circular strokes of green for the trees, the yellow for the shore, and the odd black stroke indicating the surface of the water.

◄ Part of the commercially unsuccessful series of Norwegian paintings, both of these canvases depict snow landscapes. In contrast to *Norwegian Landscape, The Blue Houses* (1895), this painting has a more complex arrangement. Rather than taking a viewpoint of the buildings as a part of the landscape, Monet has moved in close so that they dominate the picture.

NORWAY, THE RED HOUSES AT BJORNEGAARD
1895
MUSEE MARMOTTAN, PARIS.
CELIMAGE.SA/LESSING ARCHIVE

The blocks of colors used on the buildings and the lack of architectural detail allow the geometric shapes to emerge from the canvas. The result is that the buildings become secondary to the pattern of squares and oblongs that they make. The redness of the walls is striking in contrast with the deep blue of the sky. Painted at a different time of day, there is little evidence of the rosiness that the sun causes in *Norwegian Landscape, The Blue Houses*. The contrasting colors help to emphasize the geometry of the painting.

The overall effect is one of remoteness, with no human figures disturbing the white landscape. However, there is a pervading sense of calm that is shared with some of Monet's seascapes.

▼ Painted within a year of each other, *Mount Kolsaas in Norway* and *Rouen Cathedral, Sunlight Effect* (1893) (see page 190) are each part of their own series. What is of interest here is the different approaches to the use of a single motif.

MOUNT KOLSAAS IN NORWAY
1895
MUSEE MARMOTTAN, PARIS.
CELIMAGE.SA/SCALA ARCHIVES

The painting of Mount Kolsaas is a more conventional composition in the sense that the viewer is placed at a distance from the subject and can see the entire mountain. To a certain extent the mountain is given a context, with sky above and snow at its base. With *Rouen Cathedral*, a less traditional stance is taken. The viewer is thrust close to the subject. The whole of the building cannot be seen, and little context is provided, to the point that only a small amount of sky is shown. The mountain is painted in a simpler style, comprising bands of colors that contrast and merge at different points.

The colors used in the Norwegian picture are either placed in contrast to each other, as with the green line near the base next to the purple line above it, or whirled together, such as at the tip where violet, blue, and white merge. The whole is harmonized through either brushstrokes or color.

BRANCH OF THE
SEINE NEAR GIVERNY
1897

MUSEE ILE-DE-FRANCE.
CELIMAGE.SA/EDIMEDIA

◄ The Seine, a symbol of France, features in so many of Monet's works that it
became his most used motif. In 1896 to 1897, Monet decided to use the river in a
remarkable series of paintings. In all he produced 21 pictures in the series.

What renders this series like no other is that it records the dawn on one single
motif, moment by moment, within one period. Although critics had assumed this
was what Monet was attempting in other series paintings, none of the previous
series had been concerned with the changing light within such a tight time-frame.
As can be seen in both *Branch of the Seine near Giverny* and *Morning on the Seine,
Mist Effect* (1897), the dawn on the river causes varying tones to appear and
disappear. The former has a soft blue, almost lilac color that hangs across the whole
of the painting but centralizes where the river meets the sky. In comparison,
Morning on the Seine, Mist Effect was painted a little later in the morning, when the
sun begins to rise. The blue tones are beginning to disappear and the green of the
trees, especially in the foreground, is emerging. On the horizon, the sky is starting to
glow. Although these two paintings record changes in light that are easy to identify,
the differences between other paintings in the series are less clear.

IRISES AT ESTAQUE
undated

THE CHICAGO ART
INSTITUTE, CHICAGO.
CELIMAGE.SA/LESSING ARCHIVE

⬅ In this painting we are drawn into a puzzle of flowers and foliage that dominates almost the entire canvas. There is a vast mixture of flora of different colors, which clash together to increase the overall dramatic effect of the painting. Even as a close-up of a collection of plants, there is a striking lack of detail, so that the canvas becomes a splash of color. The different colors seem to be finding different directions across the canvas, so it seems as though we are being drawn into the true, raw essence of this natural setting. Nature is a strong force in *Irises at Estaque*, and we can see this emphasis in its composition.

The cloudy deep-red flowers at the top left-hand corner of the picture contrast strongly with the cool blue-purple flowers and the green-yellow leaves. *Irises at Estaque* gives a foretaste of Monet's frequent use of red in his later garden landscapes of Giverny.

The only measure of detail is on the leaves at the bottom right of the canvas, which are accentuated by a fine line of blue shade that runs beneath them to give them some prominence. A small, almost granular effect is achieved in the top right-hand corner of the picture, giving it a sketchy quality.

ON THE CLIFFS NEAR
DIEPPE
1897

CELIMAGE.SA/EDIMEDIA

➡ The beauty of Monet's clifftop paintings lies in their simplicity. The basic elements are sky, sea, and land. No particular time of day can be attributed to them and so they are imbued with a timeless quality.

In this painting it is not the strength of the sea that is on show; instead, it is a calm image that demonstrates a softer view of nature than that present in the paintings of the Creuse. In those, Monet wanted to capture the savagery of nature; in this painting he wants to depict an equally harsh landscape—but in a gentler manner. The soft curves of the cliff as it swells into the picture and gently falls into the sea are softened even further by the pastel colors used.

The viewpoint taken from the top of the cliff is repeated in many other paintings. In some it is used to more dramatic effect than it is here. In this way the cliff pictures are similar to some of Monet's earlier work such as *Boulevard des Capucines* (1873) (see page 82). His obvious interest in differing perspectives from higher viewpoints is still in evidence with these cliff paintings. However, the earlier work is concerned with capturing the busyness of a moment. Here the impression of serenity is what is most important.

SUNSET AT VETHEUIL
1900
MUSEE D'ORSAY, PARIS.
CELIMAGE.SA/LESSING ARCHIVE

◄ When Monet moved to Vétheuil, he brought his family to a more rural town than they had ever previously lived in. Unlike their previous home, Argenteuil, there was no industry in Vétheuil, and the people who lived there were mainly agricultural workers.

This rural setting meant that Monet altered his approach to his subject matter. In this painting there is no longer the celebration of the relationship between industry and nature. The backdrop to *Sunset at Vétheuil* is the wave of hills that forms around a small collection of buildings and houses. The town in this piece is the dominant feature, with its icy whiteness standing out against the pink-blue glaze of the sky and the sea. We look out over the water to this town, and there is no sign of people anywhere.

We could compare this painting to *Vétheuil*, which Monet painted a year later. This piece provides a similar perspective and subject, although looked at separately, the paintings would appear very different. *Vétheuil* (1901) has a far richer palette of greens, yellows, and golden browns, unlike the blue-gray and pinks of *Sunset at Vétheuil*. The image seems quite cold and ghostly, although it can be seen as quite serene at the same time. *Sunset at Vétheuil* displays a unique use of color, which forms a wonderful soft haze across the canvas. Overall this painting has a glossy, glass-like effect that is utterly mesmerizing.

GARDEN IN FLOWER
undated

Monet spent 20 years of his life painting waterscapes and landscapes of his garden at Giverny. This series of works was one of his greatest artistic adventures, which he pursued in the 1890s. He created, not a garden of flowers, but rather a space filled with vibrant colors and tones, blooming from every possible corner. Beautifully crafted, this garden is a masterpiece in its own right. Monet deliberately placed matching colored flowers near each other, so that they would blossom together and provide an exciting and harmonious yet busy aspect to a new canvas.

Here, in *Garden in Flower*, we can see an incredible amount of rich green, complemented by a wonderful blue sky, unusually unclouded. In one instance, it is almost surreal, as the bright plain sky and house are contrasted with a very dark area of shadow, created by the tree looming to the left of the canvas. The trees in flower stand unusually still and upright, unmoved by any breeze. *Garden in Flower* could, in some ways, be likened to René Magritte's (1898–1967) *The Empire of Light* (1853–54). In terms of their detail, both paintings have a photographic realism, which is quite unusual in Monet's works. The brushstroke here is delicate and precise, as though the artist spent many hours completing this piece.

GARDEN AT GIVERNY
1902

ÖSTERREICHISCHE GALERIE IM
BELVEDERE, VIENNA.
CELIMAGE.SA/LESSING ARCHIVES

➡ Monet's garden at Giverny was the inspiration for many of his most beautiful experimental and treasured works. *Garden at Giverny* demonstrates the artist's ability to encapsulate an enormous beauty within the confines of a single canvas. Compositionally, the scene creates a feeling of mystery, with a partly lightless passage, framed by flowers, leading toward a house, which is mostly hidden behind a film of trees. Little blotches of sun creep through the dense woods and onto the house and flowers, but it is the dense and rich purple color that leads our eye up toward the building.

The bushes alongside the trail are scattered with specks of red and white, which repeat themselves in the window frames and bricks of the building. The same is done with the green leaves of the trees on the shutters of the windows and the door. To add a further balance to the painting, streaks of red are intertwined with the green of the foliage to continue the red theme from the flowerbed below, and above the house little patches of blue sky produce the same effect with the purple flowers. Above all, the symmetry of the painting is quite spectacular, and makes a powerful impression on the viewer.

CHARING CROSS
BRIDGE, THE THAMES
1903

← Painted during Monet's second trip to London, this picture is in the same style as the others produced around this time. The London fog is used to distort colors and cloud buildings so that only outlines appear. It reflects the color of the sun across the whole of the painting so that the canvas is transfused with a pink glow.

The unreal quality that the fog gives the painting is similar to that created in some of the water lily paintings. As with *Water Lilies* (1903), the water lilies often appear as if they are hovering over the canvas. There is no reflection in the water, and their presence is not put into any context. *Charing Cross Bridge, The Thames* clearly has a context in that the Houses of Parliament are recognizable landmarks, but their ghostly appearance does not give them a solid presence in the painting. The trains crossing the bridge are equally insubstantial, represented purely by plumes of smoke.

The difference between the two works is that *Water Lilies* is an intimate painting that forces the viewer close to the subject. *Charing Cross Bridge, The Thames* lacks that intimacy because it is painted from an obscured distance.

Claude Monet 1903

⬆ This is another series of paintings, like those of the cathedrals and Monet's garden, that were completed in the later part of the artist's life. In these, he addresses his subject again in terms of color and contrast. In some instances, the bridges in these paintings become camouflaged by the color around them. This particular piece denoted a fiery quality that was found in many of his early paintings of Belle-Ile. Monet has reverted to painting on a red-brown canvas, although unlike in his *Waterloo Bridge* (1902), here the bridge does not become consumed by its surroundings. Rather, it stands out quite boldly from them.

This piece provides an insight into industrial London, with boats steaming through under the bridge, the horizon littered with industrial buildings, and Monet successfully captures the weight of the fog. Overall, he creates quite a dark and dreary perspective of the city, without the romantic quality that we can detect in other such paintings of Waterloo Bridge.

The brushstrokes are quite lavish around the curves of the bridge, compared to the smaller and more strategic ones used to constitute the water in the foreground. Meanwhile, the industrial buildings floating in the distance appear as silhouettes, as though they are shadowed by the deep color of the sky.

WATERLOO BRIDGE, GRAY DAY
1903
NATIONAL GALLERY, WASHINGTON, D.C.
CELIMAGE.SA/LESSING ARCHIVE

⬅ Painted during one of Monet's trips to London, this picture is in a similar style to the others that he produced around this time. The London fog is used to distort colors and cloud buildings so that the canvas is transfused with a pink glow. The unreal quality that the fog generates in this painting can also be seen in some of the water lilies series.

This image has a magnificent and powerful presence, with the parliament buildings silhouetted in dark black, set against the backdrop of a fiery red, billowing sky. The water has been painted to a high level of realism, with the minute waves of the water defined on its surface. The sky occasionally beams a shaft of light through, so that the tone of the red clouds can be mirrored on the water's face.

Although we are viewing this painting obscurely from a distance, there is nonetheless a striking yet unexpected intimacy that is caused by the colors used. The red sky, in particular, because of its turbulent quality, can be likened to that found in some daring religious artworks. The parliament building also, with its glaring presence, has a threatening aspect.

THE PARLIAMENT, LONDON, STORMY SKY
1904
MUSEE DES BEAUX-ARTS, LILLE.
CELIMAGE.SA/LESSING ARCHIVE

LONDON,
PARLIAMENT, SUN
BREAKING THROUGH
1904

MUSEE D'ORSAY, PARIS.
CELIMAGE.SA/LESSING ARCHIVE

▱ The Parliament paintings were among the more controversial from Monet's trip to London, because Turner had successfully included the Houses of Parliament among his paintings of London scenes. By choosing London as a subject and including in the series landmarks already painted by such a respected and acknowledged master as Turner, Monet was deliberately defying the artist, and laying down a challenge. He believed that art had progressed since Turner's day and wanted to prove that his own method of painting was superior.

In *London, Parliament, Sun Breaking Through*, Monet experiments with placing buildings near water and suffusing their connection with an eerie light. He repeated the perspective and content of this painting in *Parliament at Sunset* (1904), although the two paintings differ considerably in terms of the lighting effects used. Both depict the same scene, but at different times of the day. Monet did the same thing with his Rouen Cathedral paintings. Both series map the changes in the appearance of a building under varying conditions.

Water Lilies

WATER LILIES

undated

MAHMOUD KHALIL MUSEUM,
CAIRO.

CELIMAGE.SA/LESSING ARCHIVE

◄ In 1883, Monet rented a house at Giverny, Normandy, where he was to live until his death in 1926. Here he painted scenes and details from his garden for the next 20 years. His deliberately constructed garden became the source of inspiration for the majority of the paintings, and it is these waterscapes from Giverny that have become the artist's most famous and frequently discussed works.

Monet began the series of water lily paintings in the late 1890s. His first major group of garden pictures had a similar approach—he took a single subject and studied it intensively, focusing on it from various viewpoints in an attempt to portray it with differing perspectives, depths, and colors.

Between 1904 and 1908, Monet completed more than 150 paintings of the lily pond in the Japanese garden, and each year he began a new group with a different perspective. These paintings were giant canvases, which became larger and less focused toward the end of his life, when his sight began to deteriorate badly.

Here, we address the surface texture and detail of the water on the canvas, rather than simply focusing on the lilies, although both aspects of the painting are artistically inviting.

Monet commendably displays the elegance of his garden and the lilies, as they sit calmly on the water's surface. This was often, if not always, the prevailing feature of these paintings. The land and air were simply mirrored in the water, as it extends to the corners of the canvas. He draws us directly into the scene, while creating an air of stillness and timeless beauty.

WATER LILIES
undated

MUSEE DE L'ORANGERIE, PARIS.
CELIMAGE.SA/LESSING ARCHIVE

⬆ From 1900 onward, Monet became increasingly focused on painting his lovely garden at Giverny. Most if not all of his canvases were consumed with the swarms of color, water lilies, and Japanese bridges that were to become the most celebrated subjects of the artist's long career.

This piece is aesthetically stunning but also calming, with its predominant crystal blue-purple water, which embraces the lilies that float randomly across its surface. There is no perspective given to us in this painting, but we become completely lost and transfixed by its sheer size and depth of color. *Water Lilies* exemplifies what it is that we celebrate about the artist: his ability to stun his viewers with the breathtaking beauty and inherent harmony of his canvases.

Looking closely at the painting we can observe the subtle detail of the ripples generated by the slow motion of the lilies. In some areas, Monet has applied a fine line of color to emphasize the direction of the water's movement. The tones of the green plant hanging into the water are also repeated in its reflection and the random spots of pink and yellow are like little lights or fires that stand out against the placid blue water.

WATER LILIES
1907

MUSEE MARMOTTAN, PARIS.
CELIMAGE.SA/LESSING ARCHIVE

➡ There is a sense of suspension about many of the water lilies paintings, particularly in those in which water is the base to the composition, with no land or sky above it. The viewer is being suspended in this strange place where the surroundings have been dispensed with, and all that remains is a world of water. In *Water Lilies* we can just make out the reflection of the trees in the background, and perhaps the small fire of color creeping between the two willows is a sunrise. This provides a tepid yellow that acts as a subtle blanket over the canvas. The color scheme of this painting is like that of many of Monet's later garden paintings of the Japanese bridge.

Aesthetically these paintings abandon the cooler palette of Monet's traditional works and begin to explore the depths of fiery reds and yellows across the canvas.

The painting overall appears quite surreal. The water lilies cast no shadows or ripples on the water, so that they seem to float above a mass of liquid, which itself conveys a solid appearance, such as we would expect to find on land. They are also arranged in horizontal patches across the water, which can be likened to the shape of clouds in the sky.

Claude Monet

WATER LILIES

undated

MUSEE DE L'ORANGERIE, PARIS.

CELIMAGE.SA/LESSING ARCHIVE

⬆ Despite the strength of the blue color, this piece is instantly recognizable as one of Monet's water lilies series. Its horizontal composition is very familiar, as are the lilies themselves.

Monet returned time and time again to the garden at Giverny for inspiration. Between the years 1903 and 1908 he produced many canvases of water lilies, 48 of which were exhibited by Durand-Ruel in 1909. The series has been commended by contemporary critics for its astounding beauty and unique, harmonious quality.

In all of these works, Monet's main focus remained the surface of the water. We can see this intention here. He has dispensed with any representation of the land or sky, and the water is painted in such a way that it is impossible to gauge its depth, so it becomes a very flat canvas.

WATER LILIES

1907

CELIMAGE.SA/LESSING ARCHIVE

➡ There is a sense of suspension about many of the water lily paintings, particularly those that depict water without land or sky above it, as this painting does. The viewer is suspended in this strange place where surroundings have been dispensed with and all that remains is the world of water.

The 1907 painting is a prime example of this world of water. The reflection of clouds can just be made out, and what appears to be the reflection of willow trees appears on the left and right. By filling the canvas entirely with water, the planes of the water and of the canvas have become one. The water lilies are carefully laid in horizontal lines in both this picture and *Water Lilies* (1914–17) (see page 232).

Both the 1907 and the 1914–17 paintings are intimate for Monet because they not only represent his own private garden but also his peculiar vision of that garden. By having a subject that is so intimate, Monet pulls the viewer into his own experience of the painting. The brushstrokes in the later works become progressively broader, which was primarily a result of Monet's failing eyesight.

WATER LILIES
1914–17

◄ In 1914 Prime Minister Clemenceau urged Monet to work on a larger project, which became a formal state commission in 1916. This was for a set of large canvases depicting water lilies that would be displayed together permanently in the rooms of l'Orangerie in Paris, so that all of the walls in the two oval rooms were completely covered by them. It was intended that this would enable the viewer to become encapsulated by the nature that was the inspiration for the work. Between now and his death this was to be the main preoccupation of Monet's work.

The paintings were destined to be hung in two basement rooms of l'Orangerie in Paris. They were hung together all the way around the two oval rooms so that the viewer is completely surrounded by the water lilies. This style of painting extends to the viewer the artist's experience of the subject. It was the ultimate resolution of all of Monet's series work.

A comparison between this intimate painting and the earlier *Walking near Argenteuil* (1875) demonstrates how far Monet's style had changed. The earlier landscape is open, balanced and keeps the viewer at a distance. The use of horizontals is common to both paintings but *Water Lilies* forces the viewer close to the subject so all that is visible is the flower in a background of water. Nothing else exists.

WATER LILIES
1914–17
MUSEE MARMOTTAN, PARIS.
CELIMAGE.SA/LESSING ARCHIVE

➡ We can see from this painting how much Monet's style has changed. A large painting, *Water Lilies* forces the viewer to confront the subject, so that all that is visible is the flower in a background of water. Nothing else exists.

We can see that areas of color have been clipped from the edges of the canvas, although this may have been as a result of Monet's increasing problem with cataracts, rather than through any deliberate intention. However, *Water Lilies* still retains the inherent harmony and compositional balance that we associate with all of his earlier works. This is an aspect of Monet's work that remains strong throughout his artistic career.

The palette in this artwork is quite strong and dark compared to some of the earlier water lilies paintings. The green of the reeds is painted thickly, vertically, and confidently upon the canvas, as is their reflection in the water. This can be compared to the surrounding area of the painting, where golden-yellow and purple-blue have been applied more softly and smoothly around the reeds. The opposition of the two colors at different ends of the painting gives the impression that the green reeds are stretching beyond the constraints of the canvas, and the purple-blue color used at the base of the plants gives a sense of depth to the water.

➡ Like others in Monet's series of flower paintings, this depicts the plant in isolation. Unlike others, however, this picture does have a variety of colors and shadings as background. There is the merest hint that other plants are present, particularly on the left-hand side, where the blue brushstrokes may represent other plant leaves.

The flowers erupt from the central bush of the leaves and are painted without any detail to the flower head. Once again Monet is striving to give an overall impression rather than to represent any specific detail. The brushwork was quickly and roughly applied, and the same technique can be seen in *Water Lilies* (1914-17) (see page 234), painted at the same time. This technique has the effect of blurring the central image so that the colors merge. However, in *Hemerocallis*, the plant can still be seen in isolation from its surroundings. In *Water Lilies* the flowers were painted onto a background of water which becomes part of the essence of the flowers; the downward strokes on the surface cut across the water and the flowers.

The colors used in the painting are vibrant, testifying to the problems that Monet was encountering as a result of his cataracts. The strong red and the yellow in the background indicate this.

WATER LILIES AND
AGAPANTHUS

1914–17

MUSEE MARMOTTAN, PARIS.
CELIMAGE.SA/LESSING ARCHIVE

◁ *Water Lilies and Agapanthus* reveals two types of plant from Monet's garden at Giverny in near isolation. Probably the most dominant feature of this work is the color, which is quite minimal, yet extremely effective. The murky blues, yellows, and greens add to the image of the plants' solitude, although the choice of palette and its treatment balance the two flowers. The agapanthus petals are trimmed with a light blue, which complements the yellow of the lilies wonderfully. In juxtaposition to this, the additional height granted to the agapanthus means that they engage more readily with the viewer, which inevitably makes them the main focal point of the piece.

The detail in *Water Lilies and Agapanthus* is found more through the use of color than through any additional brushstrokes to mimic shade or features. Instead, we notice on the flower heads how Monet has touched the tips of the petals with a very light blue, which, set in contrast to the surrounding darker palette, makes it appear as though they are touched by a source of light. A similar method is used with the water lilies, the color of the water around their green pads becoming significantly lighter and bluer. The bulbs of the flowers are also painted quite brightly in comparison to the murky water around them.

◄ During the production of this painting Monet's cataracts were getting progressively worse. His sight was so poor that he had to read the labels on the tubes of paint in order to decipher which colors they were. However, *Water Lilies at Giverny* is proof that his artistic dexterity had not been compromised.

The artwork demonstrates a varying use of strong vertical, and broad horizontal brushstrokes to show the reflection of the trees in the water and to provide the detail of the lilies, which appear suspended against the lake's surface. The dark green tone used for the tree lends an effect of deepness, especially when set against the paler lilies. These seem to rise from the surface of the canvas, and the picture has a sense of drama and frenzy. It is as though the painting has been composed of a series of layers, and the different brushstrokes suggest that a sense of urgency plagued the artist as he worked.

One of the significant aspects of this work is that it successfully demonstrates the way in which Monet was able to paint the same subject in completely different ways. We only have to look back as far as 1907, to *Water Lilies*, to see what a change the artist and his work have undergone.

WATER LILIES

undated

METROPOLITAN MUSEUM
OF ART, NEW YORK.
CELIMAGE.SA/LESSING ARCHIVE

⬆ Here Impressionism seems to be taken to the extremes of abstract art. This painting was obviously produced toward the end of Monet's life, when his sight had been distorted by the worsening of the cataracts in his eyes. The entire canvas has come under the influence of one color, which quite unnerves the viewer, who is unable to rest upon a particular aspect of the painting. Instead, the lilies are submerged in this band of color. Only very small spots of blue and green-yellow creep out from under the blanket of red-pink. At the same time, however, *Water Lilies* is also made quite powerful through this application of color.

Compared to Monet's other water lilies paintings, such as *Water Lilies* (1914–17) (see page 232), the lilies themselves are not very detailed. The color technique used in this painting could be compared to *Waterloo Bridge* (1902), in which the subject itself is almost lost in the color. Both these paintings, however, are quite romantic. The color seems to represent an emotion of the painter. In the case of *Waterloo Bridge*, Monet tries to capture what he referred to as the "envelope" of light that seeps from a subject and surrounds it, giving movement to a static object. A variation of this innovative technique has been applied here.

**THE JAPANESE
BRIDGE AT GIVERNY
1918–24**

MUSEE MARMOTTAN, PARIS.
CELIMAGE.SA/LESSING ARCHIVE

➡ It is easy to map, through the Japanese bridge series, how the cataracts in Monet's eyes became rapidly worse, and how they had such a dramatic effect on the work that he produced toward the end of his career. Cherry and purple red parade across the width of this canvas as random spirals of color. They bear a weak resemblance to those of the Japanese bridge in Monet's garden.

The Japanese Bridge at Giverny is rich in color, although the piece lacks tone. The bridge is visible only because of a change in the brushstroke, which becomes horizontally curved along the width of the canvas where, from his previous paintings, we know that the bridge should be. Unusually for Monet, there is a large amount of white, which creeps through between the bold strands of color. Another noticeable aspect is the thickness of the paint and the brushstrokes. Under the bridge these become shorter and thinner, to represent the water, whereas running alongside the right of the canvas, they become longer and are thickly applied, to represent the hanging willow tree that we also remember from his earlier paintings.

245

THE JAPANESE
BRIDGE AT GIVERNY
1918–24

MUSEE MARMOTTAN, PARIS.
CELIMAGE.SA/LESSING ARCHIVE

➡ This painting shows a dramatic change in color and composition from Monet's earlier waterscapes. It also provides a deep contrast to another painting produced of the Japanese bridge in the same period, titled *The Japanese Bridge*. Here a delicate blend of green and cool blue has been replaced with a violently intense spiraling of red, yellow, and orange. Even the method of brushstroke in this later piece is far less exact, and creates a very different impression and mood of the garden.

Produced toward the end of Monet's life and career, *The Japanese Bridge at Giverny* was completed at a time when he was suffering from a severe visual impediment. Despite this, however, the effect is absolutely breathtaking.

There is loose definition where the bridge crosses the water, but there is still the strong definition of tonal variation. Certain areas of the water are touched by a gentle white and creamy yellow, which, against the angry, lush green, gives a definite depth to the painting.

The contrasting red-green palette is also used in this piece, so we can still see Monet's fascination with the effects of color. *The Japanese Bridge at Giverny* is very much alive and in motion, in contrast to the stillness of some of Monet's earlier waterscapes.

At the left-hand corners of the canvas, color has been clipped from the edges, and we can see how Monet has produced a definite curvature, the paint sweeping in an upward and circular fashion. Contrasting directions of brushstrokes elsewhere across the canvas continue this theme.

THE ARTIST'S HOUSE
SEEN FROM THE
ROSE GARDEN

1922–24

BAVARIA BILDAGENTUR.
CELIMAGE.SA/LESSING ARCHIVE

◄ Cataracts had distorted Monet's vision since around 1908, and his sense of color had been disrupted. The effect of the cataracts had been to make the world appear as if he were looking through a yellow lens. As they grew worse, his vision became browner and browner.

This painting, one of the view that Monet painted of his house at Giverny, as seen from the rose garden, is evidence of that effect. The colors that dominate are yellow and red, with very little blue in the picture. It is not easy to identify any subject in the painting, but the chimney and part of the roof of the house are visible in the left-hand corner, painted in pink. The thick brushstrokes and extremes of color are thought by some to be indicative of the anguish Monet was experiencing because of his inability to see properly.

Monet's despair over his vision meant that he suspended work on the Orangerie *Water Lilies* paintings until he was confident he would not ruin them with his poor vision. In 1923 Prime Minister Clemenceau finally persuaded Monet to put aside his fear of the operation and have the cataract removed from one of his eyes.

THE HOUSE SEEN
FROM THE ROSE
GARDEN
1922–24

MUSEE MARMOTTAN, PARIS.
CELIMAGE.SA/SCALA ARCHIVES

➡ In this piece it is as though the colors have just been emancipated from the confines of their tubes. Reds, yellows, oranges, and greens virtually scream from the page. In these later paintings Monet ventured to the opposite side of the color spectrum, abandoning the cool blues and greens of his rather restrained palette in favor of these rich and bold reds and yellows that leap to our attention. The overall effect is a *mélange* of color, rather than a concentration on subject matter.

Monet was finding it increasingly difficult to cope with the deterioration of his sight. He tried to destroy some of the paintings that he produced during this period, when he failed to return to the style of work that he desired. Another depiction of his house was completed in the same year, shortly after the operation to remove his cataracts. In contrast to the reds of *The House Seen from the Rose Garden*, this other work exudes blue, hence the references to the artist's "blue period" around this time.

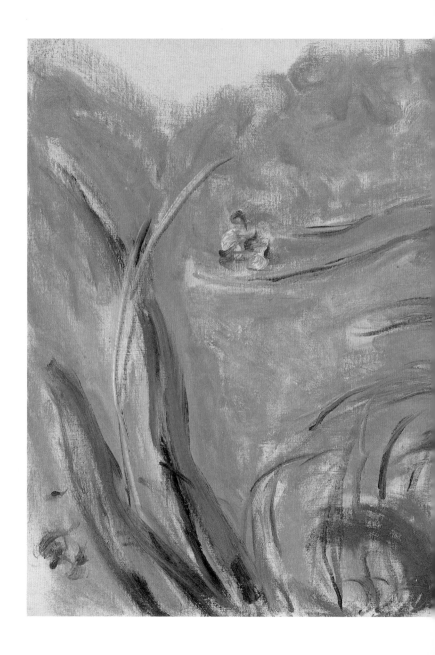

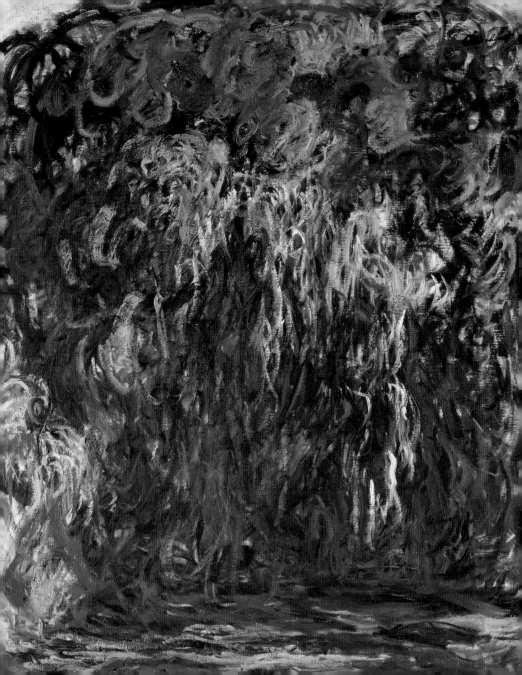

⬆ This painting is among the last that Monet worked on. Even at this late stage in his career he was still developing as an artist and trying new techniques. This is one of the many reasons why he has gained the respect of critics over the years.

With *Iris*, Monet has moved in to give an intimate view of the plant. The background is a swirl of color that is indecipherable as representative of anything in particular, so the plant exists without any distractions to the eye. It is a depiction of an iris in its purest form. Unlike his earlier paintings, it is not the amazing violet and lilac tones of the flowers that have caught Monet's eye. Instead it is the shape of the leaves; their greenness, and even some orange on one leaf, that are the focus of the painting.

What interests Monet, as can be seen in work dating back to the beginning of his career, is the grid created by the leaves; the sweep of the leaves forming horizontal and vertical lines that cross each other. The informality of the symmetry is further emphasized by the curves of the leaves, ensuring that the whole has a softened and harmonized effect.

IRIS
1924–25
MUSEE MARMOTTAN, PARIS.
CELIMAGE.SA/LESSING ARCHIVE

⬅ This is one of Monet's last paintings. His cataracts had made the world appear as if he were looking through a yellow lens. As the problem progressed, his vision became increasingly brown.

Weeping Willow, Giverny is full of bold color and a spiraling motion created through a mixture of horizontal, vertical, and swirling brushstrokes. Here, Monet depicts a weeping willow in the garden at Giverny, although the only determining factor of the tree is its color. Paintings like this have been referred to as early examples of Abstract Expressionism, rather than Impressionism. The myriad thick brushstrokes and extremes of color are thought by some to be Monet's way of expressing his internal strife about his inability to see and return to an earlier artistic style.

However, regardless of the fact that *Weeping Willow, Giverny* was produced at this late stage in the artist's life, and while he was handicapped by poor sight, it is compositionally sound, and in terms of color, the reds and greens provide a strong contrast between the willow tree and its backdrop.

WEEPING WILLOW, GIVERNY
undated
GALERIE LAROCK-GRANOFF, PARIS.
CELIMAGE.SA/LESSING ARCHIVE

Author Biographies
and Acknowledgments

Vanessa Potts was born in Sunderland in 1971. She completed a B.A. Hons in English and American Literature at Warwick University in 1992. Since then she has completed an M.A. in literature and the visual arts (1840–1940) at Reading University, from where she graduated in 1998. Vanessa currently combines her writing career with her job as a buyer for a major retail company.

Dr Claire I. R. O'Mahony has a BA from the University of California at Berkeley and an MA and PhD from London's Courtauld Institute of Art. Her specialist subject is nineteenth-century art, in particular mural decoration in Third Republic France and images of the life model in the artist's studio. She is a visiting lecturer at the Courtauld Institute and Curator for the nineteenth-century exhibitions at the Richard Green Gallery, London.

Additional and updated text by Image Select International, with special thanks to Joanna Nadine Roberts and Peter A. F. Goldberg.

While every endeavor has been made to ensure the accuracy of the reproduction of the images in this book, we would be grateful to receive any comments or suggestions for inclusion in future reprints.

With thanks to Image Select for sourcing the pictures in this book.